D1204262

Play the next Play
by June Mumme

Host Communications, Inc.
Lexington, Kentucky

www.junemumme.com

"Play the next Play" by June Mumme is published and printed by
Host Communications, Inc., 904 North Broadway, Lexington, KY 40505.
W. James Host, Publisher;
Richard A. Ford, Executive Vice President;
Eric Barnhart, Senior Vice President

Project Manager/Marketing and Promotion: Kim Ramsay
Project Manager/Production: Craig Baroncelli
Sales: Dan Leal, Tim Francis, Jaysuma Simms
Edited by Ed Kromer, David Kaplan
Editorial Consultant: Larry Vaught, *The Danville Advocate Messenger*
Design by Jeff Quire, Bill Powell
Photography by David Coyle, Victoria Graf, Breck Smither
Additional photos provided by the Mumme family
Front cover photograph by Lee Thomas

ISBN: 1-57640-023-9

Sponsors

Central Bank and UK HealthCare are proud to sponsor "Play the next Play" by June Mumme.

Central Bank

UK HealthCare
Innovation·Education·Dedication

Luther Deaton, Central Bank
President & CEO

Frank Butler, UK HealthCare
Director for Administration

Partial proceeds of this book will benefit the Markey Cancer Center. If you would like to make a personal donation, send check or money order to:

McDowell Cancer Foundation
UK Markey Cancer Center
800 Rose Street
Lexington, KY 40536

Dedication

This book is dedicated in memory of my father, William James Leishman, who passed away on June 1, 1976, and in honor of my mother, Constance Vickery. Over the past 22 years I have felt Dad's heavenly presence. He has shared in joyful moments like the birth of my children and given me strength as I conquered my most difficult challenges. Mom has been a constant force in my life both emotionally and financially as Hal and I have built his career together. They not only gave me life, they are a big part of the woman, wife and mother that I am today.

Foreword

There was once a governor in the South who was married to a head-strong woman of great beauty and energy. Upon the event of his taking office they were dancing at the inaugural ball when he quietly whispered in her ear, "Darling, aren't you glad you married me instead of Ronnie, that boy in your college class? Here you are dancing at the governor's mansion with the new governor." Without hesitating, the young first lady replied, "Why dear, if I had married Ronnie, I would be dancing with him tonight on his inauguration."

The most important day of my life occurred on a summer evening in Houston when I first laid eyes on this beautiful young woman who I knew almost instinctively would become my wife. This book is her story and our story. She is my best friend, lover, confidant and teacher. In brief, she defines me. I hope you enjoy this book — it will probably make you laugh and cry. If it creates one pleasurable afternoon for you then you will begin to understand what a quarter-century of life has been like for me. She defines me.

— Hal Mumme

Chronology

1974-1975 ....Tarleton State University, Stephenville, Texas
Student Athlete

1976.............International Harvester, Industrial Equipment Sales

Fall 1976....................Moody High School, Corpus Christi, Texas
Quarterbacks and Receivers Coach

April 1979.............Aransas Pass High School, Aransas Pass, Texas
Head Football Coach

February 1980 ....West Texas State University, Canyon, Texas
Quarterbacks and Receivers Coach

December 1981...........University of Texas El Paso, El Paso, Texas
Offensive Coordinator, Quarterbacks and Receivers Coach

April 1986....Copperas Cove High School, Copperas Cove, Texas
Head Coach and Athletics Director

January 1989 ....Iowa Wesleyan College, Mt. Pleasant, Iowa
Head Football Coach

February 1992 ....Valdosta State University, Valdosta, Georgia
Head Football Coach

December 1996 .....University of Kentucky, Lexington, Kentucky
Head Football Coach

11

First and 10 — The Beginning Years

"My favorite down! Ultimate in possibility thinking. We can score in the next three downs." — Hal Mumme

I gazed through the windshield into a future that opened as wide and full of possibility as the sprawling Texas landscape that was rushing by my father's car. It was August 1972, and my parents were driving me the five hours from our home in suburban Houston to my new life at Louisiana State University.

Like most fathers about to leave their little girls alone at college, my dad had a few words of wisdom for me.

"Stay away from the football players," he warned.

Then he hugged me warmly, and headed home.

I had never been very interested in the game of football; it always seemed boring when Daddy watched it on TV. But LSU had a great team and I enjoyed every minute of the excitement and activities that football weekends promised. Game Day was a premier social event. Before that first season even started, I had received invitations from six different boys for each of the upcoming home games. My dates would pick me up as much as five hours before kickoff. The entire day was a grand party, and everyone was invited. For me, the football game was merely an insignificant but necessary centerpiece to a weekend of social events, the boring host to a fabulous bash.

So it's no surprise that I never dated a football player during my two years at LSU. I never even met one.

About that same time, a young wide receiver named Hal Mumme was receiving a different dose of fatherly advice. "Don't marry someone you can live with," Clay Mumme told his son. "Marry someone you can't live without." Hal, hopefully, listened to his father.

I didn't listen to mine.

One summer Saturday in 1973, Hal Mumme swam into my life. Almost. I was working as a lifeguard at Ponderosa Forrest pool in Houston, Texas. As I sat watching the shallow end, this tall, trim, good-looking guy paddled up to me and suavely asked, "What does it take to be saved around here?"

I gazed at this Adonis, transfixed by his beautiful blond hair — until I remembered that stupid line he had just used on me. I chose to ignore this brash young man and moved to the next guard station. It was the last I saw of him that summer.

A year later I was guarding the deep end on a warm, beautiful night when this fair-haired, good-looking guy ambled along the pool, laid his towel down slowly, and dove in. I was curious. During my break, I asked the receptionist at the check-in gate for his name. She told me it was Hal Mumme. What an odd name, I thought. He looked familiar, though. I wondered if this was the same guy I had shot down the previous summer.

Hal's deliberate routine continued for several days. I watched him out of the corner of my sunglasses and, predictably, he pretended not to be interested. One of the other lifeguards thought he was cute and began flirting with him, which annoyed me to no end. But Hal didn't appear to take much interest. Our stalemate might have continued indefinitely had Hal's younger brother, Jeff, not finally intervened. One day Jeff walked up to me, introduced himself and then introduced me to his big brother. Within an hour, Hal asked me out on a date. I accepted.

To my dismay, Hal suggested we attend a World Football League game. Though I appreciated the invitation, I quickly made it known that I didn't care for football. I much preferred playing sports to being a spectator. In high school, I swam and played on the soccer and field hockey teams. I was a junior varsity cheerleader for basketball, which was pleasant enough to watch. But football didn't have the same pace or constant scoring to hold my interest.

Hal offered to take me to a concert instead.

Now my idea of going to a concert was packing a picnic dinner, spreading blankets on the grounds of an outdoor amphitheater and listening to the melodic music of one of my favorites: Chicago, the Carpenters or Three Dog Night. Growing up in Scotia, N.Y., a small town in upstate New York, I went to concerts at an outdoor theater in nearby Saratoga. When we moved to Houston in 1971, I had never been to an indoor show. And I still had never been to an indoor concert when Hal took me to see the Guess Who on our first date that summer of '74.

I didn't like what I heard. The ear-shattering noise and smothering smoke overwhelmed me, and I asked Hal if we could leave. Quickly recognizing my discomfort, he suggested we go for a pizza. And we spent the next several hours getting to know each other.

This suited me well. I looked at this first date as more of an interview anyway. For me to consider a relationship — or even a second date — I would first have to determine whether Hal met my qualifications. Physical appearance was important to me; but I had already concluded he was attractive. With 6 feet 2 inches of athletic build, and that blond hair, Hal fit the bill. But even more important was intelligence, background and ambition.

Education was vital to both of us; Hal was a senior at Tarleton State University and I was a junior at LSU. We both were raised in upper middle-class families. And it was clear that Hal had no shortage of ambition. Only it wasn't the kind of ambition to which I was accustomed.

I grew up in a corporate family. My dad worked for General Electric in Schenectady, N.Y., alongside most everyone in town. In my youth, work was synonymous with GE. Hal never dreamed of clawing up the ladder in Corporate America. He never cared that businesses can offer stability, career guidance, continuing education, job security and promotions based on achievement. His course would be a different one — coaching. Hal had dreamed of coaching football since he was 11 years old and organizing neighborhood games. Now the only thing he wanted to do was teach young men the game of football. I quickly realized how different our perspectives were.

I believed that teaching is a noble profession. I also knew it didn't pay very well.

But this was Hal's passion. He thrived on responsibility and desperately wanted the chance to pave his own career path, always dreaming that, one day, he would get to showcase his ideas at the major college level.

I was determined to marry a businessman. I explained to Hal that I would never marry a football coach. But he was persistent. That first date — I mean, interview — concluded with Hal driving me home and escorting me to the door like a gentleman. Before I said good night, he asked me for a second date. I accepted. After all, he met most of my qualifications. I decided to give him a second interview. But then he left abruptly — without so much as a kiss! I knew there was an attraction, so I thought this was strange behavior. Much later, when I asked Hal why he had been so coy that first evening, he replied, "Because I knew I wanted to marry you."

Courtship is a series of evaluations. Hal had easily passed the first test. He knew how to treat a lady. He was a kind, caring young man who made me feel special when I was with him.

So, though I was convinced a relationship with a future coach could never go anywhere, I still found our time together a pleasant way to spend the summer. I did conclude, after only our second date, that Hal was arrogant. Supreme confidence is a trait that has served him well throughout his career. He has always believed his ideas are better than everyone else's — and he has the conviction to follow them.

I found Hal's incredible self-confidence and strong opinions irritating, and decided to put up every roadblock imaginable to discourage his affection.

For a date with me one Saturday, Hal drove five hours from his parents' vacation home on the beach near Corpus Christi. When he arrived to pick me up, I explained that I didn't feel like going out that evening. He asked me if I was sick. "No," I said, "I'm just not in the mood to go out."

Hal was hot. Thinking I had another date, he decided to call another girl, and took her out. But he kept calling me, despite the trials I laid before him. The next several dates would severely test Hal's patience. His invitations included a movie or dinner, which only lasted until 8 or 9 p.m. Being a gentleman, Hal would always ask me what I wanted to do next. I decided if he didn't have something planned for the rest of the evening, there was only one place for me to go.

"Take me home," was my standard request.

So Hal would take me home. Our parents found our cat-and-mouse relationship amusing, but never expected it to last.

But Hal was persistence personified, and proud of it. Determined to win my heart, he asked me to spend the weekend with his family at the beach near Corpus Christi. My accepting the invitation changed the course of our relationship. Hal was vying for some uninterrupted time to convince me that his intentions were honorable. That weekend at the beach, he first told me he wanted to spend the rest of his life with me. Marriage? I was confused. I didn't understand my emotions.

Now that Hal's intentions were on the table, we would need time to let the relationship develop. Marriage was a huge step; divorce was not part of my game plan. I wanted to be sure. It helped that Hal was a person of deep Christian faith. Though he was baptized a Methodist, his family did not attend church often when he was growing up. But during high school, Hal renewed his dedication to God, and began participating in the Fellowship of Christian Athletes.

My own deep faith was nurtured early in life through my family and church. My parents were devout Roman Catholics. We went to mass every Sunday and had extensive religious education. My mother gathered all of us children to pray before sending us off to school each day. My father would lead us in the blessing before our nightly family dinners. And then Daddy would end our day by saying our prayers with us before tucking us into bed. I have grown to appreciate the strength I have received from God through prayer.

While we dated, Hal and I often discussed our beliefs and began attending my church together. Faith has always been the key to our relationship — advice we share with our children today.

We went out nearly every night that summer, growing closer with each passing week. Hal's pursuit finally culminated on the day of our wedding; we were deeply and passionately in love. To this day, Hal prides himself on convincing me to marry him. He says it was the best recruiting job he's ever done. And he still refers to me as "the girl in the red bathing suit," recalling our unusual poolside courtship, when I was a lifeguard and he was a smitten young man, coolly trying to catch my eye. So we began our life together. Hal was 22 and a wide receiver at Tarleton State. I was 20, and had completely ignored my father's advice on that day he dropped me off at college.

I was married to a football man.

Money was tight in the early years. Hal's scholarship paid for his tuition and books, and covered some of our room and board. But we had more expenses to cover. So Hal worked construction and cleaned a church every Sunday night. I provided childcare for several mothers to make a few bucks. My father gave us a Buick shortly after we married, which was extremely generous since he was paying college tuition for two of my sisters at the time.

Life was simple. Hal and I were young and in love; it took so little to make us happy. We rented a sparsely furnished, one-bedroom apartment in a small complex for $75 a month. It had twin beds and linoleum floors. When it was hot we found refuge in a window air-conditioner. When it was cold we huddled around a solitary space heater. Once, I locked myself out and a neighbor I had never met offered to help. This lanky man with cowboy boots and a 10-gallon hat suggested that we try to open my door with his key. I figured this was a stupid idea, but had nothing to lose. To my surprise, it worked! Every door in our low-rent apartment complex had the same lock! It's a good thing we didn't have much worth stealing.

Hal and I learned to have fun with little money. When we wanted a treat, we'd search the apartment for errant coins and claim the deposit on our soft drink bottles. Once we had scraped together enough spare change, we'd head to the Sonic Drive-In for a couple foot-long chili dogs, then return with our feast to the apartment to watch the Saturday night movie on TV. From time to time, we fondly relive those happy days with a trip to our local Sonic (which still makes a great foot-long, by the way).

That fall I showed my true lack of football knowledge when I first went to see Hal play. My younger sister, Nancy, had to explain the basic rules of the game: Each team gets four chances to make a first down. As long as they continue to make a first down, they keep the ball. If they don't make a first down, they kick the ball away. The team with the most points at the end wins.

So now I knew the rules. But I had another question for Nancy.

"Why is our team kicking the ball so much?" I asked.

She stood up and yelled loud enough for everyone in the stands and on the field to hear, "BECAUSE OUR GRANDMOTHER COULD PLAY BETTER FOOTBALL THAN THEY CAN!"

This was not very encouraging to hear. To make matters worse, Hal suffered several injuries in the game. Afterward, at the emergency room, we discovered he had a fractured rib, and a cut on his cheek would require stitches. Injuries did not diminish Hal's love for the game. No matter how many times he would get hurt, he always dreamed of playing — or even just trying out — for the Dallas Cowboys. Unfortunately, God didn't bless Hal with the athletic talent necessary to play at that level.

Being young and naive, I thought this would be my one and only year of football. Hal graduated from Tarleton State with a bachelor's degree in History and Secondary Education in December 1975. Just after graduation, we packed the Buick and headed toward Corpus Christi, where Hal would begin work for his father. Clay Mumme had just bought an International Harvester dealership, and began to sell farm and industrial equipment. Hal was in charge of the industrial line and earned $600 a month plus commission. Corpus Christi is farming country. And selling heavy industrial equipment in such an agrarian economy is not easy.

Among the inventory Clay inherited when he bought the business was an old backhoe that no one could sell. Anxious to move this obsolete — and space-eating — capital investment, Clay offered a $500 bonus to anyone who could sell the backhoe. The sales staff snickered, thinking it was impossible. But Hal saw not an obstacle but a possibility. A lucrative possibility. He went to work. And before long, he had sold the old backhoe by convincing a company doing roadwork in the area that it needed the equipment. Even his father couldn't believe Hal sold what none of his experienced staff could sell.

Neither success nor the promise of money could alter Hal's true passion, though. He had gone to work for his father because the job was available. But all along, he was secretly applying for football coaching positions.

I'll never forget the day that summer when Hal dropped the bomb on me. "June," he said, "I have accepted a position at Moody High School in Corpus Christi to coach quarterbacks and receivers this fall."

I was shell-shocked.

There was no discussion. Hal's decision was non-negotiable.

It was summer of 1976. My father had just died suddenly of a heart attack at age 48, we had a one-year-old son to take care of, and Hal announced he was going to coach high school football. We didn't communicate that well during the early years of marriage, but this time things really hit bottom. I refused to speak to or cook for Hal for nearly three months. I was livid. My future was to have been the American Dream: the solid, corporate job, the quaint house with the white picket fence — June and Ward Cleaver! And now Hal was giving up a bright future in sales to coach football.

After his dogged attempts to make up with flowers and gifts dragged on for months, I finally relented. The Catholic Church taught me as a child that marriage was one of the seven sacraments. I strongly believed then, as I do now, that marriage is a life-long commitment, and I am no quitter. So I decided to trust that the man I chose to spend the rest of my life with had made the best decision for our future.

Surprisingly, my father had grown to support Hal's dream of coaching, as long as he aimed high. "Be the best," he told my husband. "And don't rely on selling insurance as a backup plan."

I will never know what Daddy had against insurance as a profession.

My mother was more concerned, mostly about our financial stability. She grew up in a generation when a successful woman was one who married well. Understanding the demands of parenting, she encouraged all her daughters to stay at home to raise the children. Hal's coaching would mean I would have to contribute to the family's income.

Never having known any football coaches, my family also didn't believe the job required much intelligence. They thought Hal was far too bright to be wasting himself on coaching.

News of this career change was not received well by Hal's parents, either. They wanted him to remain in the family business, thinking it would mean a better life for us. Clay's dealership was very successful and it afforded him a comfortable living. The Mummes had a beautiful home in the Corpus Christi Country Club, expensive cars, a deep-sea fishing boat and several investment properties. This was the life I wanted. I hoped that someday Hal would purchase the company from his dad. But this was not to be.

Instead, we moved far and wide to follow Hal's career path. Since our wedding day back in 1974, we have lived in nine cities, four states, five apartments, one townhouse and 11 houses. We've been more mobile than a military family.

Nobody said it would be easy. Daily life for a coach's family means that Daddy isn't home very much. Whether in the high school ranks or in the NFL, coaching is far from a nine-to-five job. The hours are long. And for most of the football coaches toiling out there, the salaries are low. It's difficult to balance the family budget, and the wives accept the responsibility of providing the care for the children.

To coach football in those early years, Hal also had to coach a second, or sometimes third sport, teach high school history, and even help drive the bus on occasion. On nights he wasn't working, he would go to meet college recruiters, tirelessly working to establish a name for himself.

Meanwhile I watched my three sisters get married and move into nice homes. They were living the life I had dreamed of.

Hal's ambition, a quality I once found so attractive, was taking him away from us far too often. He wanted it all: a great marriage, great children, great career. And he spent much of our first decade together struggling to balance those priorities. It was my job to give him an occasional wake-up call to make sure he remembered what was most important.

Family was everything to me. Hal and I both grew up in tight-knit homes where family members spent a great deal of time together. Holidays were always special because relatives joined in the festivities. Our parents were central to us both. The values we learned growing up have become the foundation of our parenting with our own children.

My father married the love of his life. William (Bill) J. Leishman grew up in Scotia, a small town in upstate New York. Connie D'Orazio was raised about five miles away. The two began dating while attending separate Catholic colleges in Albany, N.Y., Dad at Siena and Mom at St. Rose. After a short courtship, they married and began raising six children. Daddy always said a big family motivated him to be successful. And he was. After working 20 years for General Electric in Schenectady, the company asked him to manage a plant in Houston. It was 1971, my senior year of high school, when we moved to Texas.

My parents were such wonderful role models for me. They were so much in love. One time when we were kids, my sisters and I discovered the love letters that my dad wrote during their courtship. It can be difficult to imagine your Daddy as a hopeless romantic, but I still can. Even at age 48 he was still taking my mother on dates. Before one, Mom was showering and Daddy was in a playful mood. So he turned off the hot water heater, laughing giddily at his mischief. Mom wasn't so amused by her suddenly icy shower, but she really did enjoy the attention, even after all those years. Tragically, their life together ended just days later, when Daddy died of a heart attack. I will always strive to match the love and closeness my parents felt for each other.

Ours was a happy home. I was the second of six children born between 1952 and 1960. My older sister, Chris, graduated at the top of her class at Scotia High School before we moved to Houston. Now she lives in Nashville and is a Certified Public Accountant. A year younger than me is Nancy, who now lives in Augusta, Ga. Nancy has the friendliest, most contagious personality you've ever seen; it's no wonder she was voted homecoming queen in high school. My youngest sister, Mary, has lived overseas for more than a decade. Her experiences in Argentina, Malaysia and Indonesia have contributed to her enormous confidence and enthusiasm for adventure.

Tom is four years younger than me; he's a strong and independent man who owns his own business in Houston. And Mick, the baby of the brood, is a corporate man, working for a company in New Orleans. Outnumbered by the females in our household, Dad, Tom and Mick formed a club to help them cope — "The Buddy Babes."

Growing up in a large family was wonderful, and a tradition my siblings and I have continued. We have already produced 13 grandchildren — six girls and seven boys — for my mother to dote on.

Hal's story is similar to mine. His mother, Hallie, and father, Clay, were high school sweethearts in San Antonio. They married shortly after graduation. During the war Hallie worked at a radio station while Clay served in the South Pacific. When he returned and launched a successful career, she stayed home to raise the children. Hal was the oldest of three. His sister, Pam, lives in a small town outside of Corpus Christi with her husband and three children. Jeff, the youngest, sells real estate and performs with a Christian band in Corpus Christi.

Hal's family roots trace back to our new home — Kentucky. In the late 1800s, brothers Harry and Sam Clay were raised in western Kentucky before moving to central Texas. Harry Clay married and had one daughter, Tommie, Hal's grandmother. Tommie married Walter J. Mumme in 1920. Tommie and Walter were determined to keep the Clay name alive, another tradition that lives on today. Everyone knows their son, Harold — Hal's father — by his middle name, "Clay." Hal's middle name is also Clay. And our son is Matthew Clay. Three generations and over a century after Harry and Sam Clay left the Commonwealth for Texas, their descendent became the head football coach at the University of Kentucky. History has come full circle.

Hal and I have been blessed with three beautiful children — Matthew Clay, Karen Elizabeth and Leslie Marian. All were born in Texas, but in different cities. By our 12th wedding anniversary, the lean early years were about to change for the better. That year, 1986, Hal accepted the head coaching and athletics director post at Copperas Cove High School. It was a major turning point not only for Hal's career, but also for our family. For a dozen years, I had managed the home and children almost by myself. Now Hal had more time — and more will — to help.

I also took more time to watch Hal coach. His rapport with the players was amazing, almost magical. For the first time, I began to understand why Hal does what he does for a living. For the first time, I began to support Hal's chosen career. He was truly born to coach. And now that he was earning more money, our mostly financial struggles were beginning to dissipate.

Collegiate coaching was on the horizon, with more responsibilities and worries. But fortunately, the game and rules have changed over the past decade to allow coaches more time to be with their families. Recruiting used to be an all-consuming endeavor. There were so many scholarship spots to fill that coaches would sometimes sleep in front of a recruit's house to get the edge on signing day.

But the NCAA has cut Division I scholarships to 85 per team, down from 95 when Hal began collegiate coaching in 1980. Division II scholarships have dropped from 45 to 36 today. There weren't many recruiting rules to worry about in the old days. But now contact has strict limits, and college coaches are required to document telephone calls and meetings of any kind with prospective players. Recruiting is so closely regulated that Hal was unable to attend any of our daughter Karen's high school football games because of conflicts with the stringent regulations. I didn't think it was fair that our children's experience suffered for their father's position, but it was only a minor drawback to a positive trend.

I never begrudged Hal for doing whatever it took to be the best coach possible. He was a purist; teaching and leading young men was his gift. He was so much more about passion than a paycheck.

But I had passions of my own. I always wanted to be the best mother possible to our three children. If I had little help early on, it only forged my independence and confidence. Motherhood is a privilege and a duty. The values I pass down through my children will be my legacy. I accepted the responsibility to create a stable family life for the children even as we moved so often.

Hal sometimes misunderstood the attention I devoted to our children. He began calling me a "smother mother" because I spent so much time and energy on the kids. I preferred the term "Super Mom." I knew that no one could take better care of my children than me. This dedication to the kids sometimes tested my relationship with Hal, as it did when Matt played for Hal at Valdosta.

In 1996, Matt was the backup quarterback behind senior star Lance Funderburk, a good bet to win the Harlon Hill Trophy, Division II's equivalent of the Heisman. I knew Lance had seen little action the year before when he was the understudy to Harlon Hill-winning Chris Hatcher. So I didn't expect Matt would get much playing time in just his sophomore season. But Hal told me Matt would log plenty of playing time in '96, then have two years left to lead the team.

The season opener was against Gardner-Webb in Boiling Springs, N.C., a long bus ride away. Gardner-Webb had a mammoth team, and it looked like we had a long afternoon ahead of us. But Valdosta took control of the game early, and by the middle of the third quarter, we were cruising, 42-16. The win was in the bag. Other parents in the stands began asking me why Hal wasn't putting our son in the game. I waited patiently, thinking he would send Matt in at any moment. But as time lapsed, so did my patience. From the stands I caught Hal's eye and silently mouthed, "put our son in the game."

He ignored my request. The final score was 42-19. Matt didn't play a down.

After the game, Hal was pleased with his team and smiled broadly as he approached me for his traditional victory hug. But he met a cold reception. I was infuriated. How could he have not played Matt, our first-born and only son? What was he thinking? I was too mad to form words, but my stern face said it all. Hal knew what my silence meant. It has always been my weapon of choice when we clashed. My silence spoke volumes.

Calmly, Hal explained that Matt was warming up to go in, but Gardner-Webb managed to sit on the ball the entire fourth quarter, so he never got the chance. But I wasn't buying what Hal was selling. I knew it wasn't his tendency to let a team chew up the clock like that. I can't remember how many times I've heard him instruct defensive coordinator Mike Major to either "hold them or let them score." Neither happened this time.

Hal left the matter with me unresolved, and went to the locker room to discuss the situation with Matt. Meanwhile, the players showered, grabbed their box dinners and filed onto the bus for the trip home. On board, the situation escalated. I challenged Hal's decision-making on the football field, which prompted him to send Matt and I both off the bus and give us an old-fashioned chewing out. This was a rare outburst; I can think of only a handful of times he's every raised his voice at me. But he felt it was time to explain, in no uncertain terms, the chain of command in matters of football.

But I was not shaken from my opinion. My instinct was to protect my offspring, a trait that inspired my boss at Valdosta Mall to start calling me "Mama Bear." I believed Hal should have found a way to play Matt, and that was my final stance.

The uneasy stalemate cast a pall on the bus. Everyone knew all was not well in the Mumme family. Valdosta's athletic trainer, Jim Madaleno, described the nine-hour bus trip home as "awful." The tension was excruciating. I usually rub the stress out of Hal's neck after a game. This time he got nothing. I was on strike to protest my son's handling.

When we arrived at 3 a.m., Hal stomped off the bus, hoisted his bag and strode away quickly, staying 15 feet ahead of me. We went to bed angry. The next day we were still barely speaking to each other. Hal finally broke the silence, questioning my commitment to him. "Do you love your kids more than me?" he asked.

"Oh, so how do you measure love?" I argued. "Do I love you one cupful and the kids two cupfuls? They're your children, too!"

Suffice it to say we survived this test of wills. Looking back, Hal says he regrets not letting the opponent score so Matt could have received some game experience. It would have been worth the trouble just to avoid the quarrel. Should of, would of, could of. We always learn the hard way.

Our marriage has always been one that could withstand a fierce argument. Eventually, we always make up. And I like that part the best.

These days, I give Hal a lot of attention, especially since our two older children don't live with us anymore. We treasure our time together and choose to be with each other as much as possible. I now accept that Hal must spend a lot of time on his career if he hopes to advance. I have also come to forgive him for his absence in the early days; he had so much ground to cover. Finally, at Copperas Cove, he realized how much of Matt's and Karen's lives he was missing. Since then he has been a great daddy, spending all the time he can with the children.

Now we are best friends, which is not to say the romance is gone. Not by a long shot. Hal never hesitates to profess his love for me publicly, a special gift I treasure more than any gem. Romance has always been an important part of our marriage. Simple things have meant so much to me. I remember the day Hal planned a special dinner while I was the marketing director at Valdosta Mall. Anyone who has ever worked in the retail industry can tell you the day after Thanksgiving is a big one. The official opening to the Christmas shopping season, special promotions and bargains galore make this the biggest shopping day of the year. Since I was coordinating those special promotions, I spent an exhausting day at the mall while Hal stayed home with the children. When I wearily trudged through the door late that night, Hal surprised me with a welcome touch of romance. A candle-light dinner for two was set at the table. And the kids were nowhere to be found. I was enchanted by this romantic man (who just happens to be my husband).

I remember daydreaming that I'd marry a guy like this. Like all long-time couples, we have had our share of challenges. I remember taking those marriage vows so long ago — for better or worse, for richer or poorer, in sickness and in health... The priest never said anything about football.

When Karen came home in May 1997 for support after breaking up with her latest beau, she told me, "Mama, I want to find a guy and be married like you and Daddy." She wanted to know when I decided to marry Hal. I thought about it for a moment, then gave her an answer she didn't expect. "On our 12th wedding anniversary," I said.

That was the one at Copperas Cove, when Hal finally found time for his family.

Poor Karen! I'm afraid my revelation shattered her perfect image of marriage. Like most young girls — including me — she grew up believing your wedding day was the beginning of "and they lived happily ever after."

It hasn't been that simple. But Hal and I are working on "happily ever after." Our love has only grown through the trials we now laugh about. It has aged over 24 years like a fine wine.

We have rarely exchanged presents on anniversaries, birthdays or Christmases, choosing instead to spend whatever money we had on the children. We don't need gifts to remember special days; we choose to celebrate each day of our marriage.

I guess it shows. In 1995, friends from Iowa, Linda and Charley Walsh, invited Hal to speak at an independent banker's convention. Hal went to the podium and began by introducing me. "This is my lovely bride, June," he announced. "We've been married for 21 years. I married her for passion and we've been going strong ever since."

I turned 10 shades of red. I couldn't believe he said that, even though it was true.

2nd and 9 — Moving Forward

"OK, we gained ground, but not much. We still have three downs for possibility thinking. Rome was not built in one down. Do not panic — just play the next play."
— Hal Mumme

I have little interest in the technical side of football. Hal tells me to quit watching the ball. The only time I'm able to follow his advice, though, is when our son Matt is playing. Then, like any mother, I only watch him.

At times my ignorance of the game's minutiae has been a blessing. It protects me from having to explain why Hal did this or didn't do that. Having to say I don't understand the game sometimes delivers me from uncomfortable situations.

It has never been — and never will be — my job to tell Hal how to coach or what plays to run. Early in our marriage I gave myself a simple job description: support his career. Most people are struck by Hal's inventive use of Xs and Os, his out-of-the-box football strategy. But my fascination with his vocation has always been of a more sociological nature. I'm most intrigued by the unusual relationships forged between Hal and the assistant coaches, the coaches and the players, the team and the community.

I asked several friends to help me define Hal's relationships with players and coaches. But they had no easier time groping for words to define the indefinable. These relationships are rooted in so many intangibles — integrity, discipline, teaching, love, motivation and so much more. Rather than attempt to explain this relationship, I just tell people to watch Hal during a game or practice. The way he interacts with the young men is wonderful, beyond definition. I am so proud of the work he does.

I suppose UK Athletics Director C.M. Newton gave the closest description of Hal's gift that I've heard. "He can coach," C.M. said. It sounds so simple, but means so much.

It wasn't always so simple. During the first two decades of our marriage, Hal's career was inching along — in the right direction, but not very quickly or easily. In those early years, Hal would have to make rash career decisions based on fleeting opportunities available that instant. It took time for me to understand and appreciate this type of competitive career path.

Hal hadn't played for a major college football team. He hadn't worked for a well-known Division I coach. Without the pedigree of some of his colleagues, his upward mobility was more of a challenge. He would have to accept jobs at schools looking to rebuild their programs with limited resources. In short, he would have to take jobs that many coaches wouldn't even consider.

We packed up and moved so many times that I often felt like a pioneer woman on a never-ending wagon train. Only twice during our 10 moves — to Texas-El Paso in 1981 and Kentucky in 1997 — did we have the luxury of hiring a professional moving company.

The rest of the moves were our responsibility. For such a

volatile profession, coaching didn't seem to offer much to help the incoming or outgoing coach's family. There weren't moving clauses in most of Hal's contracts to cover real estate fees or moving expenses.

When he accepted an offer from a new school, Hal would go immediately to begin working. I was left behind with the children to pack our belongings and sell the house.

While I was caring for babies and working to make ends meet, Hal was building the foundations of his career. In addition to coaching and recruiting, this meant hours and hours spent studying film, attending coaching clinics, and observing role models like Lavell Edwards at Brigham Young and Bill Walsh of the San Francisco 49ers.

Hal always saw the purpose of this endless work. I did not. I was discouraged, to say the least. Hal was spending all his time and energy on his career. Meanwhile I was expending every bit of my time and energy on raising the family and earning enough money to subsidize Hal's modest income.

During our first 14 years of marriage, Hal had two winning seasons: 1976 and '81. Fortunately, though, he was an assistant coach most of those years, making few decisions that would decide the outcome of games. So he escaped much of the blame for those trying seasons.

Losing was no fun, but Hal learned much from those years. He was always thinking, writing and reading about football, or about subjects that could be translated to football. No time or place was off limits to Hal's study. In a restaurant, he would stop what he was doing to jot down a play on a napkin. Any available piece of paper would do.

Whenever this happened I felt ignored. "This is my time," I would remind him. "Can't you leave football at the office?"

Hal would explain that he just needed to write down a thought before it left him. He made out these random football epiphanies to be so critical that I made it my duty to save every napkin and scrap of paper on which he had scribbled. But as the accumulating scratch notes threatened to overwhelm our house, I began throwing them away. I even asked Hal if he minded. No, he said. Once he wrote down a thought it was forever etched in his memory.

To this day Hal will take a moment to note an idea on any available shard of paper, at any time. I just have come to understand and accept this quirk of his personality.

Accepting Hal would have been tougher had he not always shared his career goals with me. Because coaching opportunities come and go in a flash, it was important to have a plan before the offer came. Hal only applied for jobs at schools that would move his career forward according to blueprint. But we never knew exactly where the plan would take us.

One thing was never a factor in the early years of Hal's career: money. The opportunity was always more valuable than the income to Hal; he always accepted coaching positions where he could perfect his skills while continuing to learn. But this did affect our family.

Fortunately my parents helped out graciously. We had no car payment thanks to my dad's wedding gift of the Buick. My mother covered my college tuition and books, bought clothes for our children and helped with other expenses when we were in a pinch. My stepfather helped pay our medical bills. They all made a huge investment in our family, and I will never forget their incredible support. In truth, the money they gave us allowed Hal to take so pure a path throughout his coaching career. Because pure often translated to poor. Hal's first job, coaching quarterbacks and receivers at Moody High in Corpus Christi, paid just $9,000 a year.

I was willing to work to boost our income. But I had not finished my degree and found it impossible to get a good-paying job. I finally found work as a substitute teacher. But Matt was just two years old, Karen was a baby, and both were often ill. After childcare expenses, medical bills and taxes, we didn't see much of the $30 a day I made teaching.

Still, I wanted to work and continued to be a regular substitute at a Corpus Christi junior high. The school's assistant principal, an ex-high school football coach, gave me a hard time about my husband's coaching at Moody.

"Hal made a poor decision," he said. "He'll never amount to anything."

I can still remember how deeply that upset me. Even though I wasn't totally sold on Hal's chosen career, he was still my husband and I would vigorously defend him. I have never forgotten what that assistant principal said. It was the first of many times I would hear Hal challenged.

While he was at Moody, Hal interviewed for two head coaching jobs near Houston. I hoped he would get one of these so we could move closer to some of my siblings and my mother, who had remarried a Houston lawyer and banker named Charles "Dick" Vickery. Instead, Hal got his first head coaching job at Aransas Pass High School, the hub of a fishing community on the Gulf of Mexico that billed itself the "Shrimp Capital of the World." The year was 1979. Hal was 26 years old. He would make $13,000 annually.

Early on at Aransas Pass, a couple of boosters took us to a game at Texas A&I (now Texas A&M at Kingsville). A&I was a small-college national power. Before the game we chatted with other boosters in the crowded trophy room under the stadium. It may as well have been the Dallas Cowboys' thrown room, I was so thrilled. I wondered if Hal would ever make it to that level.

But we had a ways to go. Like any first-time coach, Hal made mistakes at Aransas Pass, and the team went 1-9. Community support was poor, but the fans hated losing. After the second defeat, we awoke to hear a group of students egging our house. Hal chased them away, then went right to work washing the mess off the wall. It was my first — though far from my last — encounter with disgruntled football fans.

But Hal's resolve was never shaken by detractors. He always looked ahead to a better time. That first season he struck up a friendship with Bob Brush, the defensive coordinator at West Texas State University. Because the school had a small recruiting budget, Bob would stay with us when he was working in our area. Soon Bob recommended Hal for a full-time position at West Texas State.

The school's head coach, Bill Yung, was coming to our house to conduct the interview over dinner. Hal went to the airport to pick him up and they spent about a half-hour talking on the way. I had no idea what they had discussed as we sat down for the meal. After Coach Yung shared several football stories, the conversation shifted to the matter at hand.

"Are you sure you can meet your expenses and feed your family on $500 a month?" he asked Hal.

I couldn't believe my ears. I smiled as I fought back the tears. Was this a nightmare? We had two small children at home. It didn't take a mathematician — or a football coach — to realize the numbers didn't add up. But money was never an issue when Hal made a career decision, no matter the hardship.

I was still upset the next day, and called my mother for advice. "Mom," I asked. "How do I say, No. We are not going to do this?"

"You can't just do that," she replied. This was not what I wanted to hear.

At Aransas Pass Hal's annual salary was $13,000. Now it was going to drop to $6,000. And there was no discussion about it. Before a West Texas State booster paid for us to visit the campus, the decision was made. So we took the opportunity to acquaint ourselves with the town of Canyon. During the visit, we met the rest of the coaches and their wives at Bob Brush's house. After dinner the coaches all went back to work. I couldn't believe it. But the other wives explained that this was the way it would be. They turned out to be right.

I went to bed that night alone, tired, cold and seriously questioning our — I mean, Hal's — decision. Even Don Davis, the offensive coordinator, tried to talk him out of taking the job as he drove us to the airport the next day.

"This job will be too hard on your family," Don warned. "Don't take it."

But Hal didn't listen. For 10 months of coaching quarterbacks and receivers, he would be paid $500 a month, without benefits. In the summer, he would earn additional money raising funds for the football program. For the first of two times, we cashed in Hal's teacher retirement to cover the costs of the move.

The school let us use a donated old Cadillac. It made such an awful racket that Matt would beg me not to pick him up from kindergarten with it. But it was all we had, so Matt learned to deal with the embarrassment.

This was a busy time for me. Back in Aransas Pass I had started a sewing business. My grandmother had taught me to sew when I was a kid, and I made most of my clothes when I was growing up. I found that most women were willing to pay someone to do this time-consuming task for them. So to help make ends meet, I opened shop in Canyon. Matt and Karen were small enough to share a bedroom, so the third bedroom in our house became my sewing room.

To build my client base, I ran a daily advertisement in the newspaper and visited every clothing store in town to solicit work. With my trusty, albeit noisy, old Cadillac, I was able to offer pick-up and delivery service as well as expert alterations.

My business took off. I provided services for every clothing store and dry cleaning business in town. I hired another coach's wife to help me keep up with the demand. Before long, I was making more money in a week than Hal made in a month. During this time I took classes toward my college degree in the mornings while Karen went to preschool. In the afternoons I took care of Matt, Karen and another child while I tried to sew. But I had to do most of my sewing work at night, after I put the kids to bed. I sewed seven days a week, often until 1 or 2 a.m. to finish orders due at 8 the next morning. I was proud of the business I had built. I loved to sew and didn't mind the hard work. I even did some not-for-profit jobs on the side, creating little cheerleading outfits for my girls as we moved from school to school. I was often weary after a long day's toil. But it was a good kind of weariness, a weariness that comes from accomplishment.

Hal was accomplishing a good deal, too. West Texas State went 5-6 that year, with some great wins. The highlight was an early season victory against a powerful Oklahoma State team coached by Jimmy Johnson, who would go on to lead the Dallas Cowboys and Miami Dolphins.

That September afternoon was a scorcher. With temperatures sweltering above 100 degrees in Stillwater, Okla., the artificial turf was like a sizzling green griddle. Johnson chose to attire his team in their cooler, white jerseys so West Texas would be forced to wear the sun-soaking dark uniforms. It didn't matter, Coach Yung told our team. We would be proud to wear our school colors.

Oklahoma State was coming off a 7-4 season that had earned Johnson Big Eight Coach of the Year honors. The Cowboys were a huge favorite in the season opener. West Texas State, on the other hand, had dropped its first game to McNeese State the week before.

After the first quarter, West Texas led, 13-0. I was at home, sewing and following every play on the radio. Bob Brush had created an excellent defensive plan to stop Oklahoma State's earth-moving running attack. And Don Davis' air corps was coming up with big plays.

In the end, West Texas held on to win the 20-19 thriller. It was the biggest victory in the school's history. I was so proud that I framed the newspaper article about the game. It hangs in our house even today. I still have the game program, too.

That first season at West Texas, Hal was considered a full-time coach, though he received only part-time pay. But when another coach left, he began receiving a full-time salary. Now he was making $16,000 a year. The increased pay meant even more responsibility for Hal, and even less time for his family. He often stayed at the office watching film and talking football with Don Davis until the wee hours of the morning. Don really took him under his wing and taught him so much about the game.

The coaches' wives would get to make one trip with the team each year. In 1981 we went to the Nevada-Las Vegas game. The team rolled the dice and beat the host!

After the game Hal and two other assistants, Larry Hoefer and Mickey Matthews, strode like conquering kings down the glittering Vegas Strip, smoking big cigars and basking in the victory. But the moment could not last. They all soon went their separate ways. Today, Hoefer coaches at Texas Tech and Matthews at Georgia. But it was a wonderful moment, the kind you can never relive, but will never forget.

The team had a great year and finished 7-4. My sewing business was doing even better. With Hal's raise and my increasing income, we were able to buy a $50,000 house just before that '81 season. Life was good.

But six months later everything changed. It was only 10 days before Christmas when a neighbor called to ask why I didn't tell her we were moving.

Moving? We weren't moving, I told her.

"Turn on the television," she said.

The news was reporting that Bill Yung had been named head coach at the University of Texas-El Paso.

I tried to call Hal at the office but couldn't reach him. Finally, several hours later, he phoned.

"We're moving to El Paso," he announced. He was coming home to pack and then leave immediately.

"What about Christmas?" I asked incredulously.

"Oh, we'll work something out," he replied.

I was deflated. I had squirreled away $600 from my business so Hal and I could go on a belated honeymoon to San Antonio. Instead, I would have to use the money to fly Matt and Karen to my mother's house in Houston for the holiday. Hal met us there on Christmas Eve.

Once there, I did my best to swallow my disappointment and focus on the excitement of Hal's new job and another new experience for me and the children. By now I had decided to flourish no matter where we lived. Hal has never been responsible for my happiness. True happiness is a choice that can only be found within oneself, not in where one lives or what one owns. My happiness comes from my faith and my relationships with the people I love.

My husband left the day after Christmas to begin recruiting. I returned to Canyon to pack up our life and sell the house we had owned for just seven months.

Hal's new position was promising. Because Don Davis was staying at West Texas to become the new head coach, Hal was promoted to offensive coordinator at UTEP. He would now bring home $33,000 a year.

None of this seemed so important on Matt's last day of school in Canyon. His class threw him a farewell party. And when we picked him up, Matt looked sad.

"They all hugged me," he said, "and they think that they're never going to see me again."

Hal and I looked at each other. We knew the kids were right. This was just a difficult part of our life I had to accept.

In March, we moved into our new house in El Paso, a town just across the Rio Grande from Mexico. El Paso sits on an arid landscape filled with rocks, cacti and tumbleweed. This is a land where 10 inches of annual rainfall is considered a pretty wet year. It took some getting used to, but we grew to appreciate the desert's spare and subtle beauty.

We had no problem making new friends in El Paso. Many of our fellow parishioners at Queen of Peace Catholic Church had children the same ages as ours. They attended the same school and made their First Communions together. And because our social life revolved around the activities of our kids, we all became fast friends.

At 29 years of age, Hal was the youngest offensive coordinator in the country when he started at UTEP. Actually, the entire coaching staff was young, but it made up for a lack of experience with boundless energy and enthusiasm. Hal always said recruiting was no problem for that bunch, but admits a lack of coaching experience hurt them at times.

UTEP lost a lot of games. The administration's goals for the program were simply not realistic given the resources available. Coach Yung had been promised many things that never materialized. There wasn't enough money for proper recruiting or travel. The equipment and facilities were sub-standard. The team didn't have a weight room. And despite the blazing desert heat, the athletic dorms weren't even air-conditioned.

While Hal was learning to recruit the hard way, I decided it was time for me to complete my college education. I became a determined, full-time student. But as soon as I started, I became pregnant with our third child, Leslie. With two young children at home, another on the way, and Hal's demanding schedule, I was forced to put my plans on hold once more.

For the wife of a coach, the football season is not the ideal time to have a baby. Luckily Leslie was born on a Thursday in October 1983, the day before UTEP would travel to Colorado Springs to take on Air Force. The doctor induced labor so Hal could be present. When he had to leave the next day, I understood. By then I knew his absence was a part of my life I couldn't control. Just like with people of business, this sort of demand comes with the territory. Unfortunately, the world doesn't stop when a baby is born.

I tuned the game in on my little radio and listened from my hospital room that Saturday. We lost. We always lost. After that trying season, I begged Hal to apply for other jobs, but he was loyal to Coach Yung.

And he was determined to recruit a good team. Hal's region

was Dallas and Los Angeles. During the season he would fly out Thursday night to watch high school games on Friday, then return on Saturday and go straight to the stadium for pre-game preparations. From December 1 until the signing date in February, Hal would be gone Monday through Friday to meet with coaches and players, visit parents and talk to guidance counselors. On weekends he would be busy meeting with recruits who came to check out the campus. And each May he would leave on an extended trip to evaluate high school juniors for the coming fall recruiting season. Because UTEP couldn't afford to fly coaches back and forth to see their families, he would be away for the entire month.

But Hal worked a short respite into his grueling itinerary in May 1984 so he could celebrate Matt's birthday with us. This unusual detour home began a chain of events that may have been divinely inspired.

That week six-month-old Leslie came down with what we thought was a terrible flu bug. She was looking awful when Hal took Matt and Leslie to the mall to pick his present. A little while later, I was laying next to Leslie when the telephone rang. It was Hal, wanting to know how she was doing.

I was thrown by this call. It seemed odd that Hal would take time to check in on a little flu. I felt something was wrong. Could this be some kind of divine message warning me to seek help? The Lord does work in strange ways.

Taking a cue from Hal's uncharacteristic concern and my own inner voice of caution, I rushed Leslie to the hospital. It was a good thing I did. The doctors diagnosed her as suffering from spinal meningitis. Spinal Meningitis Hemophilus B is an infection of the covering of the brain. It is a contagious form of meningitis that can lead to blindness, mental retardation, hearing loss or death.

Leslie's intensive treatment included intravenous antibiotics, oxygen and blood transfusions. Hal had hepatitis in college, so he couldn't donate blood. My blood type didn't match. And we were concerned about blood from banks; this was before there was reliable screening for the AIDS virus. Fortunately our pediatrician helped us find our own donor in a good friend — Bill Yung.

Leslie spent 10 long days in the hospital. Hal's parents stayed with Matt and Karen so we could spend every minute with her. This was the first serious medical crisis that my side of the family had ever dealt with. Leslie's condition was tenuous. We had to make decisions regarding treatment and then pray she would be all right while we waited. Leslie, though, is a little fighter. She willed herself to live. Today, Leslie is fine. She plays tennis and is as active as can be. Best of all, her hearing is fine.

This was the most trying time Hal and I had faced. We couldn't help but think Leslie probably wouldn't have survived the night if I had not been triggered to seek medical attention when I did.

Things didn't always turn out as well on the football field. Texas-El Paso won only seven times in 46 games during Hal's four years. His last year the team won only once. But it was a win we'll never forget.

It came against defending national champion Brigham Young and coach LaVell Edwards, who had gained national acclaim with his high-scoring passing offense. Edwards was a role model to Hal. His creative passing attack relied on brains, not brawn, and effectively changed the game. Providing a successful alternative to the "smash-mouth" style of play that relied on physical superiority, Edwards elevated football to a game of finesse.

Hal's fascination with Brigham Young's offense led to a friendship with Claude Bassett, a position coach at BYU who worked the same recruiting region as Hal. Later, Claude would arrange for Hal to study Edwards' offense from the inside.

But in 1985, UTEP shocked BYU with a dose of its own medicine. Brigham Young came into the game ranked seventh in the nation and working on a record 25-game winning streak in the Western Athletic Conference. The Cougars had not lost to UTEP in 14 years. But thanks to Sammy Garza's precision passing and a vexing defensive strategy of dropping nine players into pass coverage, we won 26-19. The Associated Press called it "one of the biggest upsets in college football history."

After the game I sat in the middle of the field with Hal after almost everyone had left. We stared at the still-illuminated scoreboard. The setting inspired contemplation.

"Why doesn't winning feel as good as losing feels bad?" I asked.

Hal explained that he doesn't just coach to win. He coaches because he loves teaching young men the game of football.

Still, it felt good to me, like an unexpected cool drink on a parched desert afternoon. I just hadn't had much experience with winning during those years in El Paso.

But our time there was invaluable to us both. Hal began to develop his offensive philosophy along with his unconventional ideas on motivation and discipline. He started to see football as form of entertainment that must compete with movie theaters, restaurants and amusement parks. And he found the high-scoring passing game the best way to offer the kind of excitement that creates happy customers.

At the same time I began to understand my own motivations and assess my talents. Since my pregnancy sidelined my college degree for the moment, I joined Mary Kay Cosmetics in 1982 as an independent beauty consultant. I enjoyed the company-provided training, and learned a great deal about setting goals, controlling my destiny and thinking positively.

During those El Paso years I also became very involved in Western Hills Day School, where Matt and Karen attended. I agreed to coordinate the school's annual fund-raising dinner, and really got into planning the big event. We shattered our financial goal.

As I took stock of my professional successes — promoting my sewing business, my work with Mary Kay and the fund raiser, I began to see a common thread of interest: marketing. I found that I thrive on the promotion of good ideas, and that my work yields great results.

I also watched how Bill Yung's wife, Ester, devoted herself to her husband, his team and the community. Using Ester as a model, I developed my own style of being a head coach's wife. And I learned to brush off some of the criticisms directed at Hal or the other coaches, where once I would let them get to me. Communities love sports and want to win. Fans get frustrated when their team loses. Then they are prone to say or do some awful, illogical things. I now understand that Hal must win to keep a job. But if he loses, it doesn't mean he is a bad person. Coaching is not the only reason a team loses, either. If the commitment to win is not supported by the school and the community, then success is impossible.

Near the end of the 1985 season I was reminded that football is as much a business as it is a game. The blade dropped November 26, just two days before Thanksgiving. While UTEP was preparing to play Wyoming in the first American football game in Australia, coach Yung and his staff were fired. After January 31, everyone would be out of job. Head coaches are often protected by their contract, but assistant coaches are guaranteed nothing, though this is changing.

After hearing about his last job change on TV, I had warned Hal that if that episode was ever repeated he would be in huge trouble. Hal remembered my threat. The first thing he did after coach Yung told him the news was call me from the locker room. The conversation was brief because other coaches needed to make the same call.

The fallout was dizzying. Just after the announcement, the team flew from El Paso to Los Angeles and on to Hawaii. Then after spending the night, they completed the trip to Australia. The wives followed several days later, but we had to fly straight to Australia, 24 grueling hours away. I already had put our house on the market, and signed an offer on the way to the airport. We would have to vacate our home a week after we returned.

Maybe it was the mounting stress that caused me to get sick about halfway to Hawaii. Whatever the cause of my illness, things only got worse when we landed. The event's promotion was a bust, and many activities had to be canceled. The food was horrible. And we even lost the game.

It was rough landing for this chapter of our lives.

Coach Yung and his staff had inherited a program that needed time and resources to rebuild. The university and community simply didn't have the patience to let that happen. Still, somehow, coach Yung's staff persuaded some great players to come to UTEP. After we left in 1987, those recruits began to win games and earn bowl bids. Players like Seth Joyner, Chris Jacke, John Harvey, David Toub, Don Sommers and Tony Tolbert all went from Texas-El Paso to the National Football League. Quarterback Sammy Garza enjoyed a long career in the Canadian Football League.

As so often is the case, the staff scattered in all directions to continue their coaching careers. Bill Yung decided to stay in El Paso and go to work for an insurance company, a position he holds today.

After selling our house, we packed our belongings again — including the Christmas tree — and moved into a nearby rental before the holiday. For Hal, finding a new job would be more difficult than ever. The United States Football League (USFL) had just folded and all those coaches were spilling back into the college job market. Nothing was happening for Hal.

The height of my discouragement came one day in a grocery store. As I wrote the check the clerk asked, "Are you still here?"

I was livid. Weren't we allowed to be in El Paso anymore?

Things deteriorated further when I came home and noticed that Hal's courtesy car was missing from the driveway, but he was sitting in the living room, unaware. On the verge of notifying the police, Hal decided to call the car dealer first. The dealer admitted he had taken the car back without notice. No call. No letter. No knock at the door.

To be treated this way was more than I could bear. It was time to leave El Paso. My mother and stepfather owned a ranch outside of Houston, which they used on weekends and holidays. They allowed us to move in while Hal searched for a job. We were fortunate to have such supportive parents. With no money and no idea when we would see our next paycheck, I don't know how we would have made it without them.

Finally our luck began to improve. While the moving van was unloading our belongings on Good Friday, Hal drove to Copperas Cove to interview for the head football coach/athletics director position at a 5-A high school, the largest classification in Texas.

Now, I should explain that football in Texas is not like football anywhere else. Communities revolve around their high school teams; they find their identity in the fortunes of those young men on the gridiron. At the time Hal was approached for the job, Copperas Cove was a perennial doormat in its district. The team lost almost every game it played. The town fathers — and mothers — were looking for no less than a savior to bring back not only the football program's success, but also the community's pride. This was no small decision.

Hal's first interview was with a selection committee comprised of the men on the school board and the school's superintendent, Dr. Richard Kirkpatrick. The committee's charge was to select three finalists from this first wave of interviews. The entire school board would then interview the final three before making a final choice.

When Hal arrived, Dr. Kirkpatrick was driving another candidate to the airport. So the rest of the committee began the interview. The more they talked with Hal, they more they liked him. By the time the superintendent returned, the committee members were touting Hal as the answer to their prayers.

They asked him to return Monday for the next wave of interviews, this time with the women of the school board included in the process. As Hal drove the two hours back to our temporary home, his enthusiasm grew. This was a great opportunity.

While Hal was heading home, the selection committee continued to meet. They were so confident they had found the only man for the job, they decided to hire Hal immediately, before the women on the board even had a chance to meet him.

So the next day, Hal was pretty surprised when the phone call came from Dr. Kirkpatrick. It was my husband's 33rd birthday, and he was about to get an unexpected, but welcome, present. The job was his. The selection committee wanted Hal to start right away, which suited me just fine. The superintendent asked us all to come to a press conference Monday in Copperas Cove. As usual, Hal took the job without asking about the salary.

We arrived for the press conference unaware we were walking straight into a hornet's nest. The women on the board were irate that so important a decision had been made without them. We couldn't have felt more uncomfortable.

To make matters worse, three-year-old Leslie tripped over the TV cables and began to wail. The board asked us to wait outside while they met privately to work things out. Media members were clamoring to know what was happening. I looked at Hal and said I was taking the children to McDonald's until things calmed down.

Eventually the women agreed to support the selection committee's decision. But they did want to ask some questions. While Hal explained his philosophy, Dr. Kirkpatrick wrote something on a piece of paper, tore the note off the tablet, and slid it under the table. With a glance at the note, Hal learned his new salary — $36,000 a year.

This wasn't much more money than Hal had been making at El Paso. But now he would be the boss; he could finally implement his own ideas for rebuilding a football program.

Hal's good friend, Mike Major, was the first to join his staff. Hal had met Mike while coaching at Moody High in 1977. Mike wasn't married back then, so he spent much of his time at our house. He'd often join us for dinner — Hamburger Helper was the humble specialty of the house — but he'd never complain. Then he and Hal would watch reel after reel of 16-mm game film projected onto the refrigerator door. Hal and Mike escalated this video-viewing ritual with an annual trip or two to Brigham Young to pore through their film library. They would need some big ideas if they were to rebuild a program that had won only 14 games in the past 12 years. Copperas Cove was the runt of Texas' 5-A schools. Because it was a military community, chances were good that a freshman would move away before he reached his senior year.

Hal and Mike began canvassing the hallways to find potential players. This active approach to recruiting worked wonders. The team went 5-5 that first year, and notched wins against two schools Copperas Cove had never beaten. The second season we went 3-6-1, and tied perennial powerhouse Killeen. The team won four times in our third year, including a victory over Temple, a team that had drubbed Cove, 70-0, two years before Hal's arrival.

Although a dozen wins in three years seems like a modest accomplishment, it felt like glory days to the residents of Copperas Cove. After years of hopeless frustration, Hal's wide-open system made the players believe they had a chance to win every week.

While Hal's career was taking wing, another of our family was launching his playing days. Matt was a seventh-grader when he first began to learn his father's system on the Copperas Cove junior high team. Under his dad's tutelage Matt learned to play football; but he also learned larger lessons about teamwork, perseverance and dedication. Hal learned a lesson, too: about a mother's concern for her son.

Texas is sweltering in August. As preseason practice began, I became concerned about Matt getting dehydrated after I read a few articles on the subject. According to time-honored routine, the players could get a drink only at scheduled breaks. I didn't think this was healthy. When I counted the number of breaks, I knew Matt wasn't taking in enough liquid. So I began lobbying for water on demand. And I was one football mom that wouldn't go away. I was certain I was right and determined to get my way. After endless badgering, Hal finally called in the junior high coach and ordered him to make Matt's mom happy, or else he was fired! Matt and his teammates would have water whenever they needed it. I was elated at my victory.

Hal had to coach the junior high team once that year when the regular coach couldn't make the game against mighty Temple. Matt was the quarterback and scored his first touchdown at the end of the game, to bring our team within one. Showing his competitive tendencies, Hal elected to go for two points and the win rather than kick for the tie. The conversion failed and Cove lost by a point. But this was a great day for everyone. We all had so much fun that the parents tried to convince Hal to coach the junior high team every week. It was a flattering offer, though Hal had to decline, reluctantly. I was so proud to be Matt's mother and Hal's wife at that moment.

But high school football in Texas has a dark side. Crazed parents and fans can take their interest to extremes, as we found out first-hand when we played Georgetown on the final weekend of the 1988 season. Georgetown was a rival that counted on Cove as an annual victory. But that year we were beating them, 42-14. With just two-and-a-half minutes to play the frustrated father of one of the Georgetown players came uncorked. He started climbing over the fence and shouting that he was going to kill Hal. My heart raced as I watched this lunatic heading onto the field. But I had my children with me; there was nothing I could do but hope and pray.

Luckily, the police quickly stopped the game and escorted Hal and the team to the locker room. Copperas Cove was declared the winner. We later learned that the man was carrying a gun.

At least we could rest easy, thankful the Police Department and the school administration had handled the volatile situation so well. But it wasn't over. The next morning I arose and went outside to get the newspaper. Instead I found the remains of a mutilated deer strewn across the yard. I was petrified. Who would do such an awful thing? I ran inside to wake Hal and pleaded with him to clean the mess before the children saw it. We always worked hard to protect them from the negative side of Hal's career, and this was about as negative as it gets.

The cleanup went unnoticed; our children never saw the hateful message left on our own lawn. But I felt violated like never before, knowing the odious thing someone had done to us — in our own yard as we slept — over the outcome of a high school football contest. It's not always just a game.

Most of our experiences at Copperas Cove were wonderful. Hal maintains he learned how to be a head coach then, facing the likes of Bob McQueen at Temple, Inez Perez at Round Rock and Johnny Tusa at Waco. All the teams in the conference had great programs and their coaching staffs spent the entire year figuring out how to beat each other.

Hal also learned how important it is to keep people informed. When you're a head coach, you can't work in a vacuum. Don Davis once advised Hal to find the place in town where all the decision-makers go for coffee, and then join them as often as possible. He figured those people were going to talk about the coach whether he was there or not, so he might as well hear what they have to say.

Don gave Hal another kernel of sage advice. He suggested from experience that it is easier to turn around a losing program if the players and fans believe the team can score.

I learned a few things, too. The football coach in a Texas commu-nity is a town leader. As Hal's wife, I wanted to contribute to each place we called home. So I got busy. I became very involved with the PTA of Matt and Karen's school. I chaired the Ways & Means Com-mittee, and coordinated the school's carnival fundraiser. To promote the event, I launched a rap contest at the school and asked the stu-dents to create and perform the lyrics that promoted the carnival. The winner would get to record the entry at a radio station, then hear it broadcast on the airways.

This promotion really got the school and the community excited. The parents generously gave their time and energy. We even hand-painted visors to thank all the volunteers, who loved the gesture and were ready to sign on again for the next year. And the carnival raked in money for the school, shattering every previous fund-raising record. Most importantly, the event fostered a spirit of friendship and goodwill among the community. I felt great about my contribution.

During our years at Copperas Cove, I also developed a greater ap-preciation for the vital role athletics play in a young person's life. Through Matt's experience, I could see how the lessons learned on the football field would benefit a young man greatly in the future. These were lessons that couldn't be taught in a classroom; sports were the perfect complement to a student's academic training.

The energy and excitement Hal pumped into Copperas Cove was contagious. The school administration and community loved him, and rewarded him handsomely for his good and hard work. By the time we left, he was earning $46,000 a year.

But after a while, Hal yearned to get back into the college game. He began applying for head coaching positions at small colleges. His friend, Steve Kazor, who was coaching the Chicago Bears' special teams at the time, suggested he apply for the open job at Iowa Wesleyan College in Mount Pleasant, Iowa. The college president, Dr. Robert Prins, had asked Steve for advice on hiring a new coach. Thanks to the tip, Hal got an interview in December.

Once again, Hal made a great first impression, and Dr. Prins offered him the job. The catch? It paid just $24,000 a year. To my surprise, Hal did something he had never done before: he turned down the job based on money. It was almost 1989, and he simply didn't think we could live on that salary.

Disappointed, Iowa Wesleyan continued its search. They still wanted Hal, and compared every candidate to their first choice. But no one measured up. Desperate to sign Hal, Dr. Prins called during the '89 Rose Bowl and offered a base salary of $30,000 annually, plus a bonus based on the number of players he recruited. This was still $16,000 less than Hal was making at Cove, but he felt it was a figure we could manage. Hal accepted. And for the second time we cashed his teacher retirement to support the move.

Matt was in seventh grade, Karen in sixth and Leslie in preschool. With the children right in the middle of their school year, we packed up again and moved to Mount Pleasant. In a hurry to get settled, we rented a house sight unseen. This turned out to be a disaster. The house was a little more "rustic" than we had expected. For example, whenever someone ran a bath upstairs, water leaked through the floor and cascaded into the room below. After four months of primitive living, we moved out.

But Mount Pleasant was a joy. The small manufacturing and farming community of 10,000 sat about 45 miles south of Iowa City and 30 miles west of the Mississippi River. It reminded me of a Norman Rockwell print, with its beautiful central park surrounded by quaint little shops, and crowded street dances on summer nights.

Hal's task was not so attractive. He would inherit a team that had gone 0-10 in the 1988 season. At the first team meeting, eight players showed up; three of them had followed Hal from Copperas Cove. After the sparsely attended meeting, Mike Major, who had made the move with Hal, set out to "get some players."

And get them he did. Mike's expert recruiting enticed 32 Texans to come north and play for Iowa Wesleyan, an NAIA school. His pursuit of perfection was a real asset to Hal and the coaching staff. To this day the two enjoy a great friendship based on mutual respect and a deep understanding of each other. Mike even accepts his unusual role as defensive coordinator in the Hal Mumme system — sometimes he must stop the other team; sometimes he must let them score quickly so the offense can get back to work.

We hadn't been in Mount Pleasant long enough to buy a house before Hal was heading back to BYU to continue his football education. So I was left to hunt for a home. Hal's pay cut didn't make it any easier. Most of the new houses were more than we could afford, and the older ones needed more repair than I wanted to tackle.

While Matt and Karen went to school, Leslie and I would drive around looking for new listings. One morning, I discovered a house I liked, and called BYU to tell Hal the news. Because I had no idea how to find Hal, I asked for Claude Bassett. Since he was away from his phone, I left a message with his secretary asking him to have Hal call me. But I didn't say why.

When he got the message, Hal went into a panic. He called immediately, fearing it must be an emergency with one of the children.

"What is it?" he asked anxiously.

"I bought a house," I replied.

"You did what?"

"I bought a house," I said again, brimming with confidence after making such a major decision on my own. I knew it was a great house, and I knew Hal would love it.

Our new home was beautiful, a 100-year-old Victorian with a circular, oak staircase at its center, the sunlight flooding in from windows all around. Leslie wasted no time staking her claim to one window that was just the right height for a preschooler.

We bought the house for $48,000 and, thanks to our low-income status, qualified for a low-interest government loan that left us with a manageable payment of $450 a month.

The previous owners had updated the wiring and plumbing, but the tacky interior decor was vintage 1970s. This had to change. I loved renovating the old house. It was an adventure. We converted the master bedroom back to a dining room, replaced the blaring orange kitchen counters and added one modern convenience: a dishwasher.

But the former owner's predilection for pumpkin orange didn't stop with the ghastly counter tops. The upstairs bathroom walls, and even the antique claw-foot bathtub, were painted orange. We kept the tub, but painted it white. On its round bottom we inscribed, "Hal, June, Matt, Karen and Leslie Mumme lived here in 1989-? Hal is the head football coach at IWC." If someone ever disconnects the plumbing and turns over the bathtub, they'll find our message.

Fixing up the old house made me feel more a part of the Mount Pleasant community. Hal had his own ways of getting connected. At Copperas Cove, he had begun a daily habit of joining the local men for coffee each morning at the Cactus Hotel and Restaurant. In Mount Pleasant, the coffee crowd gathered at Dicky's Maid Rite. Dicky's was a combination gas station/convenience store/sandwich shop that specialized in a messy confection stuffed with browned hamburger and secret spices that was to die for. Dicky's manager, Bob Lamm, was a sometimes over-enthusiastic fan of the IWC Tigers, who was once thrown out of a game for yelling at the officials too vociferously. In this football-happy gathering place, Hal laid the groundwork for community support.

And he gave those fans plenty of reasons to cheer. After Wesleyan fans suffered through a winless 1988, Hal's first squad went 7-4 in '89, and capped the season with a trip to the inaugural Steamboat Classic in Burlington, Iowa. For his miracle work, Hal was named the NAIA District Coach of the Year. The growing number of Iowa Wesleyan fans were becoming enamored with Hal's daring passing attack and aggressive choice of plays. They soon began calling him the "Mississippi Gambler" for his high-rolling ways.

Winning felt so good. No, it felt GREAT! Happy days were here at last. Beginning with that 1989 campaign at Wesleyan, Hal posted nine-straight winning seasons, and nearly extended that record in his first campaign at Kentucky. His Tigers improved to 8-4 in 1990, and returned to the Steamboat Classic. And things just kept getting better for the program. Iowa Wesleyan finished the '91 season with a 10-2 record and the school's first NAIA playoff appearance. Hal was named District Coach of the Year a second time.

All the while I was working on my own triumphs. Our move to Iowa finally gave me the opportunity to finish my undergraduate work. That first winter I became a full-time student. Hal's job at school got my tuition waived. During this round of college, I studied so much that Hal began to think I lived at the dining room table. I was determined to earn my degree, and nothing was going to stand in my way. I knew I would need every advantage — and certainly a college diploma — to overcome Hal's ambition, which actually hindered my career at times. Being married to a fast-rising football coach was no asset to my job search. I found in Iowa and several times afterward that some prospective employers would eliminate me as a candidate because they feared we might not be in town long.

Finally, in May 1990, I graduated with a 3.6 grade-point average in business administration. I was proud as a peacock.

If Hal's meteoric rise sometimes hindered my own career plans, we also made a great team. I worked with the Iowa Wesleyan booster club on many marketing and fundraising projects, and it was a great opportunity for Hal and I to pool our talents to promote the football program. I produced the game program, posters, a weekly radio show and special promotions. Hal and his team provided the rest.

I learned that a rebuilding project doesn't end on the football field. There was much more to do. We needed to solicit financial support to sustain the effort. Corporate sponsorship seemed to be the answer. So during our final season at Iowa Wesleyan, I went to work pitching sponsorship packages that included tickets, game announcements and advertising in the game program and on Hal's radio show. I was thrilled to be applying my course work to the real world.

Iowa Wesleyan was as tough a sell. The entire state is as devoted to the University of Iowa as Kentuckians are to UK. But we got through to two companies who bought into the packages on our first try — a huge success given the towering odds stacked against the project. The exercise really taught me a lesson in perseverance; my belief in Hal inspired me to keep going.

But if my corporate side was beginning to blossom, my considerable maternal instinct hadn't diminished a bit. I wanted to help make the young men playing for Hal feel special. Iowa Wesleyan was a small college, but it was expensive and there wasn't much scholarship money available. So many of Hal's players had to work extra hard. I tried to do little things to boost morale, like baking each player his own birthday cake to share with his friends. The young men loved the attention.

By our third year in Mount Pleasant, we had hit our stride. Hal had amassed a 25-10 record. His offense was churning out 43 points per game, and the defense was holding opponents to just 21. Season ticket sales and donations to the football program had increased dramatically. Even Iowa Wesleyan's enrollment was up 66 percent, from 600 students when we arrived to about 1,000. When he hired Hal, Dr. Prins had hoped a winning football program would attract more students to the school and contribute to a positive experience for the entire student body. It looked like mission accomplished. Or so we thought.

The attention all this winning brought to the program made the school's faculty and board nervous. They believed Iowa Wesleyan was focusing too much on football. Midway through the 1991 season, Dr. Prins told Hal he would no longer have a job after December 31.

Dr. Prins made no public announcement during the season. Despite the difficult news, Hal worked as hard as ever, and the team finished 10-2. Once again, he was looking for work. He thought his contract would protect him, but his friend and attorney, Gary Weigle, informed us it was too vague to be of any benefit to Hal.

I was discouraged, considering yet another move just when things seemed to be going so well. As I sat there, nearly in tears, Gary offered some comforting words of encouragement.

"June," he said, "in five years you will forget all about this when Hal is coaching at a Division I school."

I had a difficult time thinking that far ahead. I was more concerned with how I was going to pay the mortgage and feed my children.

This time an opportunity came quickly. Hal received a call from a man named Travis Bryan III from Bryan, Texas, who had concluded from a nationwide search that Hal was the best man to fill the football coach/athletics director position at Bryan High School. Travis' youngest son, Joel, was a promising quarterback in the seventh grade. And his dad wanted the best coach possible for him.

Travis Bryan II had hired the outgoing coach about 20 years earlier, and now Travis III figured it was his duty to find the next one. He vigorously courted Hal for the job, flew us all to Bryan and escorted us around downtown to build support. But another school board member had been courting another candidate at the same time, and Travis — not to mention Hal — lost the game.

I was disappointed at the time, but it was probably for the best. If Hal had taken the job, he would have felt obliged to stay throughout young Joel's high school career. Six months before Joel's graduation, the offer came from Kentucky.

Hal's job search appeared to have ended when he accepted a position under head coach Guy Morriss with the Washington Marauders of the brand new Professional Spring Football League (PSFL). The team was training outside of Orlando, Fla., but was scheduled to play games at RFK Stadium in Washington, D.C. I had my doubts about Hal's newest venture as he left Iowa to join the team with a plane ticket he had to purchase himself. I had no idea when I would see him again, or if he would even be paid. Hal's an optimist, especially when he wants something to be true. But I didn't share his enthusiasm this time. The pragmatist in me had seen too many new professional football leagues fold since we were married.

Soon after Hal arrived in Florida, the league began to flounder financially. Before it went belly up, Morriss received one paycheck. The assistants got nothing.

Fortunately, Hal had not quit looking. In late January, he interviewed for the head coaching job at Valdosta State, an NCAA Division II school in Georgia. He never expected to get the job.

The first person to contact Hal was attorney Bill Moore, a Valdosta alumnus who sat on the selection committee. "I understand you like to throw the ball," he asked.

"Yes," Hal quipped, "but not until we get off the bus."

His easy-going confidence had made a great first impression. And it only got better. Within a week Valdosta State offered him the job. When the PSFL went under a few weeks later, Guy Morriss joined Hal's staff as offensive line coach, the same position he mans today at Kentucky.

The move was a good one for all of us. We loved Valdosta, a beautiful town in south Georgia with a population of about 60,000. Valdosta State College had an enrollment of 6,500 in 1992, but quickly grew to 10,000 when it became a university in '95. The campus was one of the most charming I have seen, with its Spanish stucco buildings and red tile roofs.

After high school graduation, Karen enrolled at Valdosta State. In high school, she wasn't our only athlete. In 1992 Matt was a high school junior playing for Valdosta High. That first season in Georgia, Matt's team won the high school national championship.

Leslie had a great school experience as well at the outstanding St. John's Catholic School, run by Sister Rebecca Campbell and Sister Pauline Otegen. The secretary and principal, respectively, created an ideal environment for the children, and parents often scheduled their professional lives around school activities. Both sisters are huge sports fans and love rooting for the Atlanta Braves, Notre Dame (naturally), and now the University of Kentucky.

Valdosta State initially paid Hal $48,000 a year for his coaching duties, plus additional money for radio and television shows. And he earned it. His high-flying attack was just what the Valdosta search committee ordered. For the next five years, the Blazers would average nearly 4,000 yards passing and 35 touchdowns tosses a season. Those prolific squads still hold volumes of Division II records. More importantly, Hal's explosive teams drew record crowds. Forty victories in five-straight winning campaigns, and 35 points a game packed them in to see the hottest show in town.

The honors flooded in, too. The Georgia Sports Hall of Fame named Hal its 1994 Georgia Coach of the Year after his team went 11-2 and advanced to the Division II playoffs for the first time since the school began playing football in 1983. Eventual national champion North Alabama stopped Valdosta in double overtime of the quarterfinals. That year, quarterback Chris Hatcher won the Harlon Hill Trophy awarded to the top player in Division II.

One of Hal's best wins at Valdosta came during that 1994 season. We were playing at Central Florida — *Sports Illustrated*'s preseason No. 1 in Division I-AA. I can almost feel the smothering heat that oppressed Orlando's Citrus Bowl that Saturday afternoon in early September.

This was a money game for Valdosta State, an annual matchup against a larger school that guaranteed a healthy payoff to help finance the smaller school's football program. In theory, the larger school got an easy victory in return. And in truth, these games usually meant a loss for Valdosta State.

But that day, our team shocked Central Florida. It was the first time the Blazers had ever beaten a Division I school. After the game I escorted the school's president, Dr. Hugh Bailey, and his wife, Joan, to the locker room so Hal could present them the game ball. The Baileys were big supporters of the program.

Right after the presentation, Hal had to hurry off to the press conference. The most direct route went straight through the shower-lined locker room. I was not about to go this way.

But Hal grabbed my hand and said, "Let's go."

"I can't go through there," I protested, holding my ground. "The boys are showering."

"Keep your eyes down and don't look," Hal shouted giddily, as he whisked me away.

And that's exactly what I did! I don't know who was more embarrassed, the showering young men or me, as I sprinted through. I didn't want to find out.

What a day it was! We were on top of the world. The next year *Orlando Sentinel* sports columnist Brian Schmitz wrote:

"The Knights (of Central Florida) unveiled their brand of the popular West Coast offense... The West Coast offense took a rather untraditional route into UCF's game plan, arriving with a grits-and-gravy flavor from Georgia, Valdosta, specifically. UCF studied Division II Valdosta State's version of the offense, an edict handed down shortly after the Blazers' quick-strike attack derailed UCF 31-14 last year."

They say imitation is the sincerest form of flattery.

The good times just kept rolling for Hal and Valdosta State. In 1996, GTE Region II and Gulf South Conference picked Hal as their Coach of the Year after Valdosta State won its first conference championship. The Blazers clinched the title with a 63-30 romp over Central Arkansas in the season's 10th week. After the game, football thrills gave way to real-life drama when all-American quarterback Lance Funderburk proposed to his girlfriend at the 50-yard line, as Valdosta State students cheered him on.

Hal's teams were forged by the daunting Gulf South Conference, packed with the top teams in the southeast and some of the best Division II coaches in the country. Like the SEC in Division I-A, the Gulf South champion was always a national title contender.

In Hal's unorthodox system, Valdosta State chose to carry fewer players on scholarship instead of the 65 allowed in Division II. This left some money that — along with the windfalls from games against bigger schools — allowed the team to fly to many away games, a creative strategy Hal employed to keep his team fresh. His often out-sized teams would arrive in town rested and ready, and they usually won.

With Hal's income finally at a comfortable level and the kids busy in school, I was finally able to re-launch my career. After a pair of interviews, Valdosta Mall hired me to be its marketing director. Hal was supportive; he understood that I wanted to establish my own identity and be known as someone other than "the football coach's wife." I was tickled when Hal became known, at the mall, as "June Mumme's husband." What a welcome switch.

My job was perfect. I developed and implemented a marketing plan and budget to promote the large, regional shopping center, which had three major department stores and more than 75 specialty shops. I planned events to increase sales and traffic in the mall. In every facet of this job, I was able to draw on my education and experience drawn from years of running a small business and working for PTAs and Booster Clubs.

There were many facets. Among my responsibilities at the mall were sales promotion, merchant relations, media relations, special events, publications, decor and public relations. I coordinated fashion shows and visits from Santa Claus and the Easter Bunny. As soon as one project ended, another was beginning, so I never had a chance to be bored.

I worked closely with the local media, and often wrote my own articles. Jerry Guy, editor of the *Valdosta Daily Times*, sometimes even gave me a byline. I loved working on promotions with the local radio stations, especially WAAC, a local country music station — I'm a huge country music fan — and Power 96, which gave us a lot of free air time to promote community events.

My job demanded that I travel to quarterly corporate meetings in Montgomery, Ala. I loved having the opportunity to network and learn the business, but I hated having to listen to smug North Alabama fans remind me of their successes against Valdosta State. I felt some vindication after UK shocked the Crimson Tide of Alabama last year, and the local weather reporter announced, "There are Big Blue skies all over the state of Alabama today."

The mall position also afforded me the chance to take continuing education classes through the International Council of Shopping Centers. Sharing ideas with marketing directors from around the country was such a great experience.

I thoroughly enjoyed my stint at the mall. But after working five years, I decided it was time for a change. I had always been interested in medicine, and wanted to pursue a career in health care marketing. After a short search, I was hired in 1996 by Radiology Associates of Valdosta to direct its public relations. I took a pay cut to take the job, but I wanted to gain some experience in the health care field with hopes to someday open my own medical marketing consulting business. I guess high aspirations run in the family. Hal's not the only one who doesn't let a little thing like money stand in the way of a career move. Besides, my new job was part-time and allowed me once again to work with Hal on his radio and TV shows, and speaking engagements.

Throughout Hal's career we had made steady progress, but mainly by taking baby steps. It was like the game, "Mother May I," that I played as a child. One person was the Mother, and the rest of the group had to stand in a line and ask her for permission to advance. You could ask for baby steps or giant steps. But only Mother decided whether to grant the wish. The game took persistence, like our life in football. We were just waiting for one stingy Mother to let us take a giant leap.

We didn't know it at the time, but Mother was about to budge.

Photo Album

The Leishman children. Front Row (L-R): Christine, Tom, Nancy. Back Row: June, Michael, Mary.

June was raised in Scotia, New York, before moving to Spring, Texas, during high school.

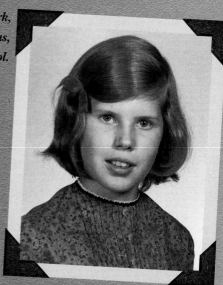

Hal lettered as a wide receiver at New Mexico Military Institute in 1970-71.

June Leishman became Mrs. Hal Mumme.

June, Hal, Matt and Karen celebrate Easter in 1981.

The long hours demanded of football coaches often place primary childcare responsibilities on the coach's wife.

Matt, Leslie and Karen joined Hal on the Sun Bowl sideline following a 1984 spring practice.

As an assistant coach at the University of Texas-El Paso from 1982-85, Hal was an instructor at the Miners' annual summer camp. Matt is in the second row, far right.

Five-year-old Karen often joined the UTEP cheerleaders in entertaining the Miner crowd.

Following in her older sister's cheerleading footsteps, Leslie roamed the Copperas Cove High School sideline in 1986.

In 1987, Hal, Matt, Karen and Leslie let everyone in Copperas Cove know it was June's birthday.

The Mummes lived in a beautiful Victorian home at 511 East Washington in Mount Pleasant, Iowa.

Prior to the 1991 football season, Hal, June and the children visited Mount Rushmore.

Despite their hectic schedules, the Mummes always took the time for a family vacation, like this trip to Ruidoso, New Mexico.

Hal's first coaching staff at Iowa Wesleyan included Mike Major and Mike Leach (second and third from left, respectively, in first row). Mike Fanoga joined the IWC staff one year later, and the three assistant coaches followed Hal to Valdosta State and eventually Kentucky.

In 1990, Iowa Wesleyan closed an 8-4 season with a 35-28 win over Olivet Nazarene at the Steamboat Classic in Burlington, Iowa.

Hal and June work hard to maintain a balance between family and careers.

Hal presents Matt with an award at the 1994 Valdosta State football banquet.

Valdosta's 1995 matchup with UTEP gave Hal an opportunity to visit with Bill Yung (right) and Dennis Richard.

Hal, June's mother Connie Vickery, June and Leslie at the Valdosta High School graduation in May 1995.

*Hal was introduced as Kentucky's football coach at a
Dec. 2, 1996 press conference.*

*Hal and his players had plenty of reason to celebrate
throughout the 1997 football season.*

In 1997, Tim Couch and Kentucky's talented wide receiver corps put Mumme's offensive philosophy to good use, setting several school and SEC records.

Coach

Please use this for Coach Hal Mummie salary

Johnny Hart

P.S. I wish I could give more

It was not uncommon for Kentucky athletics director C.M. Newton to receive notes from a fan looking to supplement Coach Mumme's salary for a job well-done.

Jubilation reigned after Kentucky defeated Alabama for the first time in 75 years.

Hal and June accept the American Football Coaches Association GTE Region II Coach of the Year Award during halftime of a UK basketball game at Rupp Arena.

June (fourth from left) attended a Kentucky Cancer Survivors' Tea at the Governor's Mansion in Frankfort in May 1998.

On behalf of the McDowell Cancer Foundation, June accepts a $5,000 check from Green's Toyota at halftime of the 1997 Kentucky-Tennessee game.

3rd and 26 — Challenges

"So the first and second downs were not so good — who cares? Great opportunity is often disguised as an impossible situation. Stay the course! When surrounded by superior forces, attack, attack, attack!" — Hal Mumme

Years ago someone shared a story about a small community in which folks were told to wrap up their troubles in a bag and toss them in a pile in the middle of town. There was a catch, however. You couldn't leave town square without taking a sack of troubles from the heap. You could choose any bag — and anyone's troubles. But after a day of bearing other people's problems, everyone chose their original bag to take home.

During our lives, we all face challenges. And though our troubles may be exhausting and frustrating, at least those troubles are our own, a constant, familiar companion. Watching Hal's early teams lose so many football games was a struggle. The times when

Hal lost his job were trying, too. And Leslie's illness was everything from taxing to terrifying.

In the past few years, my bag of troubles has runneth over with health problems of my own. But I hate to call them troubles or problems. I wish those terms could be replaced with the word challenge. Troubles suggest imminent surrender and defeat. But challenges bring out the competitor in each of us; they offer another opportunity to prove that anything is possible.

My life has never been short of health challenges. In my youth I was often ill, mostly with strep throat and ear aches. When I was four years old, a bad case of the mumps destroyed the hearing in my left ear. I still only hear with my right ear, which can cause some awkwardness in social settings. If I fail to respond to someone, it's not because I'm snobbish or aloof, but rather because I cannot hear. Crowds amplify my hearing problem. And, unfortunately, I'm often in them.

These childhood maladies only hinted at larger challenges that loomed in my adulthood. In 1994 I was diagnosed with a thyroid problem called Graves Disease. I knew something was wrong when my heart began pounding frantically and my entire body started trembling for no apparent reason. I was sick and scared. Medication regulated my thyroid output, but it was no cure. For that I would have to take a radioactive iodine capsule under the supervision of Dr. Charles Hobby, a radiologist at the South Georgia Medical Center's Nuclear Medicine Department. It all sounded pretty technical and frightening to me. But it has become as necessary a part of my life as eating and sleeping. I still take a synthetic drug called "synthroid" to replace the hormone my thyroid gland produced. I'll take it the rest of my life.

To help recover from my bout with Graves, I began an exercise routine that included a daily 10-mile bicycle ride. But this didn't turn out to be such a healthy idea. One sunny morning in late June, I was peddling around the puddles and muddy remnants of a Friday night rainstorm. As I turned a corner, the bike started skidding and flipped out from under me. In a flash I was catapulted headfirst toward the ground. I landed hard on my arm and face. The pavement was unforgiving.

I was alone and feeling like I might go into shock. There was so much blood gushing from my head that I feared I might lose sight in my left eye. Unable to see all my wounds, I tried to assess the damage by touch. I knew the injuries must be serious. I could barely move my arm. My teeth didn't seem to fit together correctly. And there was so much blood. I was sickened by the very real fear that I might be deformed forever.

I managed to drag myself to a neighbor's house. I covered my face with my hands, too numb to feel the pain.

Our neighbor dialed up Hal, and caught him just before he took the field for a youth summer football camp. He insisted we call an ambulance, but I refused. I wanted my husband, not some stranger, to take me to the emergency room. Hal suggested we go see Jim Madaleno, the athletic trainer at Valdosta State. But I told him, in no uncertain terms, that my injuries were way beyond Madaleno's expertise.

My second call was to my children. Being a so-called "smother mother," I had to make sure they were in good hands. I told Karen about my injuries, and gave her instructions about caring for Leslie. I assured her we would call as soon as we saw a doctor.

As I waited for Hal to arrive, I was afraid to look into a mirror. The doctors said the accident had dislocated my jaw and broken several bones on the left side of my face. A plastic surgeon stitched the cut above my left eyebrow and another doctor put my fractured arm in a sling. Surgery for my broken jaw and facial bones would have to wait until the swelling went down. My battered face was already turning black and blue. I would just have to keep ice on my face as much as possible to help reduce the swelling. I rested Sunday, but decided to go to work at Valdosta Mall as usual on Monday. I wanted to stay busy. Surgery awaited on Thursday, and I knew sitting at home would drive me crazy. The problem was my tattered appearance — I didn't want anyone to see me. I hid in the privacy of my office. There was no way I was going to walk into the mall looking like one of Hal's players after a particularly brutal game.

Luckily, there was no sign of concussion or brain damage, and I was thankful. The only thing permanent was some nerve damage to my upper lip and inside mouth, leaving me feeling like a dentist has numbed the area for dental procedure. Only this numbness never goes away. Ever since I have had to be extra careful with my speech.

After the accident I decided to replace the bicycling on my exercise routine with tennis. I love the sport, as do Hal and the kids. We joined the Valdosta Country Club, and I began taking lessons on the club's clay courts from John Hansen, the club pro and head tennis coach at Valdosta State.

I also began working as the public relations director for Radiology Associates in August 1996. My first day, Jackie Matthews, the office manager, introduced me to the eight physicians in the practice. Little did she know I was already acquainted with two of them: Dr. Charles Hobby had treated my Graves Disease and Dr. Robert Weiss had read my X-rays after the bike accident. "I promise you, I'm really healthy," I said, turning to Jackie. "I've just had some unfortunate experiences lately."

I figured my promise was good. After battling the thyroid disease and braving the crash, I thought surely nothing else could happen to me.

I was wrong.

October is National Breast Cancer Awareness Month, and the Radiology Associates were gearing up. It was already August when I started, and I went right to work on several projects to increase awareness of this disease. I was thrilled when the editor of the *Valdosta Daily Times* agreed to run a feature story about breast cancer on the front of the "Life Times" section.

The *Valdosta Daily Times* published my piece on Sunday, October 6, the day after Valdosta State played mighty North Alabama for the sixth time in Hal's tenure. After tying North Alabama in 1992, Valdosta had lost four-straight to their annual rival, including a heartbreaker in the 1994 playoffs. The sixth time was the charm, though, and Valdosta snatched victory in triple overtime. It was a Mumme day in that Sunday's *Daily Times*, with game coverage on the front page and sports section, and my article on breast cancer in the Life Times section.

I went for my annual physical three days later. The chief technologist at Radiology Associates administered my mammogram, a low dose X-ray of the breast that is the best tool available for detecting cancer. This is a recommended annual medical test for women over 40 — I was 42 and it was my second mammogram. The radiologist saw something suspicious in my right breast, and requested additional views. It was the first time I had ever needed a second X-ray, and I was beginning to feel uneasy.

After taking a second look, the radiologist called Dr. Hobby, who was in Boston for a meeting, to discuss the results. They decided to refer me to a surgeon they knew, and made an appointment for the next day.

I went to dinner that night with a girlfriend, so I wasn't able to tell Hal the news until about 9 p.m. But while I was out, Jackie Matthews from Radiology Associates called to see if I was alright. This message sent Hal into a panic that only worsened as I explained the situation.

I tried to remain calm and confident. I told Hal that women find breast lumps all the time, and that 90 percent of them are harmless. But nothing helped. Hal was inconsolable. When he's really upset, Hal becomes withdrawn and despondent almost to the point of depression. The more concerned he became, the quieter he got. His face turned deathly pale. That's when I knew I had to call my friend, Dr. Hank Moseley, to ask him to reassure Hal.

But Hal doesn't often worry without good reason. The next day Dr. Dal Miller, a general surgeon, examined me. I'll always remember the moment. It was exactly 4:45 on a Thursday afternoon when he gave me his diagnosis from behind his desk.

"I'm 90 percent sure it is cancer."

Cancer? I couldn't believe it! There was no history of cancer in my family. The women on both sides were known to live long, healthy, independent lives. I thought I had a genetic insurance policy against catastrophic diseases.

As Dr. Miller's message sank in further, the fear consumed me. I sat in silence, shaking, as he explained how cancer cells invade the body, and how the symptoms manifest themselves. When he asked if I had any questions, I didn't know where to start.

Was I going to die? I had so much to live for. Hal's career was finally taking off. Leslie was only 12, and I desperately wanted to see her grow up. I wanted to watch Matt and Karen get married, and hold my grandchildren someday.

My discomfort was obvious to Dr. Miller. He suggested we call Hal. I agreed, but requested that Dr. Moseley join us to help break the news to Hal, who was at football practice.

"Babe, it's bad news," I told him over the phone, trying to mask my terror. "Can you meet me at the doctor's office to discuss my condition?"

Hal was on his way before I had the chance to hang up the phone. When he arrived, we sat down with both physicians and formulated a plan. My fight would begin the very next morning on the surgery table. Dr. Miller would perform a relatively new breast-conserving procedure called a lumpectomy, in which the tumor plus a margin of healthy tissue is removed. This would tell us definitively whether the tumor was malignant.

My doctors advised us not to tell the children anything until after the surgery, when we would have more information. Matt and Karen were living at school so no explanation was required for a night away from home. Leslie was already visiting her close friend, Erica Goss. We asked Erica's mother, Patty, to keep Leslie for the night. Patty had been diagnosed with breast cancer in

March 1996 and had just completed her chemotherapy. Since it was a weeknight, we told Leslie we were going out to dinner with some NFL coaches.

It was a long night for Hal and me. I thought about the future, but also about the past. A decade earlier, I was plagued by a recurring dream in which I saw Hal holding me as I lay dying in a hospital bed. Back then I told Hal it meant I was going to die before him.

That night, lying fitfully at home, I tried so hard to picture my face in that 10-year-old dream. Was I an old woman awaiting final rest after a long and happy life? Or was I a young woman in that deathbed, about to be robbed of such a bright future? My mind spun with a maelstrom of questions. Had my dream been a premonition? Would cancer take my life?

After a sleepless, seemingly endless night, Friday morning finally arrived. I arrived at the South Georgia Medical Center at 6 a.m. Several of the doctors I worked with at Radiology Associates sat with Hal during the surgery. When I awoke in the recovery room, Hank gave me the bad news: it was cancer.

Still groggy from the anesthetic, I didn't fully digest the diagnosis immediately. I couldn't yet fathom how hard it would be to tell the children and the rest of our families, much less find the energy to fight and live.

Hal and I were facing some of the most difficult, and most important, decisions of our lives together. Luckily, there was so much going on that I was too busy to find time for any self-pity. My no-nonsense father had always discouraged pity. When one of my siblings or I felt sorry for ourselves, Daddy would have little sympathy. "Are you having a pity party?" he would say. "Is anyone coming to your pity party?"

Instead, he encouraged us to be strong and get on with the business of living.

I had little time for wasted energy. Besides, I was more worried about Hal than about myself. Not wanting to convey his fear to me, he did his suffering in silence. I know it was hard for him to imagine a future without me, just as it would be for me to imagine a future without him. So the best thing for us both was to stay busy while we decided the best path to combat my cancer.

The lumpectomy was an outpatient procedure. After I was released from the hospital, Hal took me home and then went to his office to finish preparing for the next day's game. That afternoon he told Matt about my diagnosis. Our son was understandably upset. When Hal came home, we asked Karen to come by the house before she left for a University of Georgia football game. When Hal explained my condition, Karen began sobbing. Amid her tears she said she was going to cancel her trip to the game. I urged her to go, saying I would see her when we returned from Hal's game in Arkansas. She couldn't believe I was still planning to go on the trip, as if this news would halt my normal existence immediately. But I knew if I wanted to live, then I better go ahead and do it.

A whirlwind weekend was just the thing to get my mind off physical woes. Hal called these short football trips "Commando Raids," a nod to his fascination with military history that gives him so many ideas about discipline, motivation and strategy that he parlays to coaching. The team would fly in early on game day, conquer the enemy quickly, then return on the same day.

My doctors agreed I could travel, which was great news. Being with Hal was the best medicine; he always made me feel better. And, in a sense, I was probably the best medicine for his silent struggle. We reassured each other, and didn't want to be apart any more than we had to.

Despite the doctors' okay, Karen was still shocked. But she grudgingly decided to resume her plans.

"If you're not going to stay here," she said, "then I'm not going to stay here."

I laughed and told her to go to the game with her friends.

Just after Karen left, Leslie returned home from school. Hal told our youngest that we needed to talk to her. I could see that she sensed something was wrong.

"Am I in trouble?" she asked sheepishly.

When we told her no, she started to cry.

"We're moving," she guessed. "Those NFL coaches asked you to move last night, didn't they?"

Hal and I laughed, and assured her we weren't moving. But Leslie was out of theories. It was time to tell her about my breast cancer.

To my surprise, her eyes dried immediately. "Is that all?" she asked.

Leslie had just watched her best friend's mother survive surgery and chemotherapy, all the while continuing to do the things mothers are supposed to do. Leslie was just two days from entering her teen years, but we were relieved to see her react with the simple resilience of a young girl. We wanted more than anything for her to feel safe and secure, and not worry about her mother.

Saturday, we flew to Greenville, Miss., and drove to the game at Arkansas-Monticello. The Commando Raid was a success; Valdosta rolled to a 52-24 victory. Though it was a long, tiring day for me, I was glad I went.

The weekend was only a brief refuge from medical concerns. Monday was another difficult day. We met with my surgeon, Dr. Miller, to review the pathology results. He explained that cancer grows in four stages, with stage four being the most advanced. Mine was diagnosed pretty early — late stage one/early stage two. The tumor he removed from my breast was about 2.5 centimeters in diameter, but the cancer had spread to adjacent tissue. It was critical to remove enough additional tissue to leave a clean margin where the cancer had not yet reached.

This meant I would have to undergo a mastectomy — in my case a modified radical mastectomy — to remove my entire right breast along with a section of non-protruding breast tissue that extended to the breastbone, the collarbone, the lowest rib and back toward the side muscles. The operation would also remove the lymph nodes in my right armpit.

I knew I was fighting for my life, so the removal of my breast didn't seem so important at the time. But later the loss would become a big issue with me, if not with Hal. On that day, though, I was scared. Though I terribly feared dying, I resolved right then and there to fight with all my will to survive. Hal and I pooled our energy to beat this together; we gathered our strength for the trying times we knew were ahead.

The surgery was scheduled for Friday, October 18, 1996, a date I'll never forget. No woman would. Cancer survivors use the surgery date as a benchmark to count the years of their survival — a sort of second birthday.

The day of my surgery, we took Leslie to school to make sure she'd stay busy. Matt and Karen sat in the waiting room with Hal. Karen missed a chemistry test and had to take a zero because her professor would not let her make it up, an important reality check that there are some cold-hearted people in this world. But the test was the last thing on her mind. I could sense that Matt and Karen were frightened. This was hard for them.

The team of surgeons removed my entire right breast, a good bit of nearby tissue, and 30 lymph nodes from my right armpit. Two plastic tubes were sewn into my body to allow excess fluids to drain over time.

The surgery itself was not painful. The nerves that provide sensation in the chest were severed as part of the procedure, leaving me with little feeling there. But after the surgery, my right arm throbbed from the removal of lymph nodes. Afterward, Hal and Matt sat with me until it was time for the team bus to leave for Alabama. Matt was now a sophomore on Hal's Valdosta team. Karen stayed by my side, though I spent the day sleeping.

The doctors said the surgery had gone well. But we still didn't know the results of the lymph node dissection when Hal and Matt had to leave for Alabama.

I had packed my radio so I could listen to the game on Saturday, which was a great diversion from the nurses' periodic visits to check my incision and monitor the drainage from my tubes. That morning Dal Miller came with good news. Since the breast drains primarily into the armpit's lymph nodes, the doctor explained, it is critical to check those nodes for any sign of cancer after an operation. He had found no lymph node involvement, which was a good sign the cancer had not spread further.

Hal called from Alabama before the game. When I told him the news, he was thrilled. During his pre-game talk, he shared the information with his players, who had all been really supportive of me. I was glad Hal felt comfortable telling his team about our challenges. No one ever knows when they might find themself in a similar position. The father of one of Hal's players at Valdosta was even diagnosed with breast cancer. It's rare, but it does happen. The more awareness there is, the better for everyone.

As I listened on my little radio, Valdosta cruised to a 52-16 win. During the fourth quarter, Valdosta play-by-play announcer Mike Chason sent me a heartfelt message. "June, I know you're listening," he said over the airways. "We miss you and everyone here sends their thoughts and prayers for a speedy recovery. Matt's gone in the game."

I was ecstatic. After Hal and I had quarreled so vehemently over Matt's lack of playing time earlier in the season, now I listened as my only son confidently led the offense down the field and scored his first collegiate touchdown.

The team didn't arrive home until 3 a.m. Sunday. Just as he promised, Hal sneaked into the hospital. I was feeling low, but I was so happy to see him.

"Babe, I can't look at my body," I told him. "I just can't look."

Hal kissed me and said it didn't matter to him, everything would be fine. "You'll always be my girl in the red bathing suit," he said.

Then he went home to get some much-needed sleep.

I was released from the hospital Sunday morning. When Hal arrived to help me home, I asked for his support as I prepared myself to take a first look at my body. Before the surgery I had a pair of beautifully shaped size 34 DD breasts. Now there was just one. On the other side was a hollow that extended from my collarbone down to where my right breast had been. You could see the outline of my ribs through my skin. More than 100 metal staples closed my incision, which ran from the middle of my chest, under my armpit, and toward my back, like a meandering railroad track. This was what cancer had done to me!

Hal hugged me and told me it didn't matter. I wasn't so sure.

I left the hospital that day with a chest full of staples and a pair of drains embedded in my chest. Half the staples were removed a week later and the rest the following week.

Hal patiently cleaned and bandaged my drains daily. When the time came to remove the final drain, four weeks after my surgery, my body had literally grown attached to the plastic tubing. The stitch holding it in place had to be cut before it could be pulled out. The pain was excruciating. I screamed so loud that even God could hear me, not to mention everyone in the doctor's office.

My family was very concerned about me in those days, but offered tremendous emotional support. My younger sister, Mary, even flew in from Malaysia to see me. When I saw them, I tried to present as healthy and confident a facade as I could muster. I wanted to reassure them.

But everything was not okay. Hal tried to show me through words and gestures that his love was unconditional. But he didn't know how to touch me or hold me anymore. He was always worrying he was going to hurt me. My right side did hurt, too, when I slept on it, not because of Hal.

My fight with cancer was far from finished, but I was determined to get my life back to normal. A couple weeks after my mastectomy, I began gingerly hitting tennis balls with Leslie. I couldn't hit very hard at first, but within a week I was back playing matches with a friend. I also made a point to support Hal's team, which was in the midst of a thrilling 1996 season. Six days after my release from the hospital, I was back in the stands with my sister, Nancy, cheering on Valdosta to a 42-0 Homecoming victory. I had eased back into my routine. But our lives were about to take a huge turn.

A few weeks before my surgery, Hal had received a strange, out-of-the-blue call from a sportswriter named Larry Vaught from *The Advocate-Messenger* in Danville, Ky. Larry wanted to know if Hal had any interest in the head coaching job at the University of Kentucky. Naturally, Hal said yes. But he never expected to hear from anyone at the school.

But three days after I left the hospital, Valdosta State's athletics director received a call from his counterpart at the University of Kentucky, C.M. Newton. C.M. was asking permission to discuss with Hal the head coaching position at Kentucky.

This was the big one, a true dream job at a program playing at the highest level of collegiate competition. Never in our wildest dreams could we have concocted a fantasy greater than this. We didn't believe UK would actually hire a Division II coach. But what an honor just to be called!

Interviewing for a head football coaching position is not like interviewing for other jobs. It's an exciting, emotional, exhausting and, if you're not careful, very public process. Hal and I have known every emotion that comes with the territory. We've shared the bittersweet thrill of making it through every grueling battery of interviews, only to see the job go to another candidate. And we've known the satisfaction of getting the offer. I've learned the importance of keeping the process strictly confidential for both security and sanity.

Hal agreed. He didn't want to compromise his Valdosta position by discussing a potential change with just anyone. Instead, he would confide only in his top assistants. I would trust no one but my mother and sisters with the excitement or disappointment of the outcome. Most of our friends were surprised that we managed to keep our talks with Kentucky so secret.

The process moved quickly. Within 10 days of C.M.'s exploratory call, he was in our living room with Larry Ivy, UK's senior associate athletics director, interviewing Hal. I served pastries and coffee before excusing myself to go upstairs and read.

A few moments later, C.M. called up, "June, we would like for you to be a part of this interview also. Would you please join us?"

I sat quietly on the couch listening to Hal field specific questions about his philosophies on motivation, discipline and offense. Just before they finished, C.M. asked if I wanted to add anything. I did.

"Ask the parents," I said. "Talk to the parents of our previous players, and ask them how they feel about their son's playing experience under Hal."

I know a few things about parents: first, they're always Hal's best recruiters. They adore him. And second, they tend to talk your ear off about their son's great playing experiences, but they're not likely to go on at length about anything negative.

C.M. thought it was a good idea and requested some names. We exchanged goodbyes and Hal drove his interviewers to the airport. When he returned, we nervously rehashed the meeting. At first Hal assumed the interview was only a courtesy. He didn't think Kentucky would actually hire a Division II coach. It would be the Cinderella story of all Cinderella stories. Whatever the initial intention, we both felt the interview had gone so well that this implausible tale might just come true.

A week later C.M. and Larry returned, along with Associate Athletics Director Kathy DeBoer and Assistant Athletics Director John Cropp. They wanted to meet with Hal and his assistant coaches.

The second interview went as well as the first. But Hal was distracted. We had just met with two oncologists — one specializing in chemotherapy, the other in radiation — to determine what additional treatment I would need to prevent a recurrence. I prayed I wouldn't need any at all.

Because the disease affects each person in a different way, oncologists look at each patient's prognosis before deciding what direction to take in further therapy. The doctor studies the pathology report that identifies tumor size, lymph node involvement, hormone receptor levels and the genetic makeup of the cancer. Then he or she determines the risk of recurrence, defined by statistical data accumulated from the entire population of breast cancer patients on record. From this mountain of information, a treatment plan is devised.

In truth, I didn't care about averages or statistics. I was concerned about myself, not millions of other people who had been treated for breast cancer. Just me!

There were no guarantees. But there were ways to improve my odds. The chemotherapy specialist presented my options, along with the risks and side effects of both chemo and radiation. He explained that surgery had given me a 70 to 80 percent chance of surviving without additional treatment. Chemotherapy would add another 10 percent toward my survival, and hormone therapy an additional two to five percent. So with the full battery of additional treatments, my chance of surviving breast cancer stood at 90 percent.

Hal would support me no matter what. But he told me it was my life. Only I could make the final decision. He was right, too.

You don't stay married to a riverboat gambler without plenty of gumption. I decided to request the most aggressive treatment possible, given the risk. My specialist said I needed to begin treatment within six or seven weeks of the surgery to receive the full benefit. Because Hal was in the middle of the interview process with Kentucky, we agreed to postpone until the latest possible date — December 3.

Hal felt uneasy about accepting the job, if it was offered, considering my ongoing health concerns. He offered to remove himself from contention. I knew he was sincere in this offer because he has always been with me when I needed him, no questions asked, either in person or in his prayers.

But taking his name off the search list was out of the question. We had worked too long to let an opportunity like this slip away. There aren't many major college athletics directors who would even consider hiring a Division II coach. Passing up this chance would mean yet another baby step — another low-profile small college position, or a daunting rebuilding job at a lackluster Division I program — before a school like Kentucky in a conference like the SEC would look at Hal.

I found that I wanted this job as much as my ambitious husband did, and was willing to do whatever it took to make our dream come true. Still, I conceded that we had to consult my surgeon before making a final decision. At one of my daily appointments to drain the remaining fluid from my chest area, I told Dr. Miller I had an important question and asked him to review the doctor-patient confidentiality relationship before I asked. His interest was piqued.

Satisfied I could trust him, I explained that Hal was one of the finalists for the head coaching job at the University of Kentucky. He was blown away.

"This is big," he said. "Really big. I am trained to keep medical information confidential, but this is really big."

Years ago, Dr. Miller had hoped to do his internship in Lexington, so he was familiar with the town and the school. He was ecstatic about the news, and strongly encouraged us to pursue the dream. He even helped develop a plan for my treatment in case Hal was offered the job.

With the green light illuminated, Hal got ready for his third, and final interview with UK. It took place the day after Valdosta beat Albany State, 38-28, in the first round of the Division II playoffs. This time, University of Kentucky President Dr. Charles Wethington accompanied the four who had come for the second interview. They met at the airport for convenience and privacy from the curious media hordes.

The UK contingent was late due to an interview with another candidate. They posed yet another phalanx of questions for Hal.

Then, just before they were finished, Dr. Wethington asked if he wanted to disclose anything from his past that hadn't been covered.

Hal revealed the closest thing to a skeleton in his otherwise tidy closet: his leaving Iowa Wesleyan on poor terms. Then he told them about my cancer. Everyone expressed personal concern about my health, but the panel assured him this information would have no bearing on their decision.

I wasn't so sure. They could see how much Hal and I support each other. I knew they would wonder how much time he would need to spend with me instead of rebuilding their football program, and it worried me.

C.M. told Hal they were going to take Monday to digest all the information they had gathered and be back in touch on Tuesday. During their decision day, he called Dr. Prins at Iowa Wesleyan to hear his side of the story. Dr. Prins put it as objectively as possible: Hal won a lot of games, but some people felt football was detracting from the mission of the school, so they asked Hal to leave.

Tuesday lasted forever, or so it felt. Hal stayed busy preparing to play Carson-Newman in the Division II quarterfinals, but he didn't stray too far from his office phone. Both of us waited nervously for the call.

At 6:15 p.m. the phone rang at home. It was C.M. calling for Hal.

"He's not at home," I told him, "but I'll be happy to have him return the call."

C.M. laughed and asked, "Don't you want to know?"

Of course I wanted to know! The last time we got a call like this was five years ago, when the Valdosta athletics director phoned to offer the job. Hal wasn't home then, either, but the AD insisted on telling him in person rather than sending a message through me.

But C.M. was more generous with his information.

"The University of Kentucky is offering the head football coaching position to Hal," C.M. announced, "if he will accept."

If he will accept? I paused, speechless. Then I looked up and saw Hal walk in.

"C.M., Hal is here now and I'm sure he would love to hear you repeat that message," I said. Hal picked up the phone and accepted the job before C.M. could even finish offering.

We didn't know what we were getting ourselves into, but we were thrilled to find out. C.M. flew to Valdosta the next day to negotiate a contract. Hal whisked C.M. through the backdoor to keep the sports editor of the Valdosta Daily Times, who was in the football office at the time, from finding out.

UK called a press conference for Monday, December 2, to introduce the school's new football coach. This was one day before my treatments were scheduled to begin. The plan was to fly us to Lexington right after the Carson-Newman game. C.M. asked us not to talk to the media or to discuss the offer with anyone outside of family members and coaches affected by the hire.

Even without leaks, the press was beginning to get wise. Thanksgiving morning I went outside to pick up our newspaper, and was greeted by a picture of Hal splashed across the front page with a caption billing him as the leading candidate to be named the new coach at Kentucky.

"Some secret," I thought.

The phone began ringing off the hook. Writers and broadcasters from Georgia, Florida and Kentucky all wanted a statement. We left each of them guessing. "No comment," was the standard response.

One Lexington radio station would not give up; their deejays would call daily during the early morning show. The onslaught of attention and the incessant phone calls were beginning to wear on Leslie. We finally told her not to answer the phone. I took all of the calls, saying Hal wasn't home and we had no comment. The media begged us for a morsel, citing the magnitude of the story in their desperate pleas.

"No comment," was our answer, every time.

Hal tried to keep his team focused on beating Carson-Newman. But that Saturday's game took place in Jefferson City, Tenn., not too far from Lexington. Wildcat curiosity drew plenty of hard-core

Kentucky fans to the stadium that afternoon. And Kentucky's eager media circus came in force, swelling the game's press contingent far beyond normal levels.

I sat among them in the press box that day, straying from my usual seat in the stands with the parents of our players. I relished those Saturdays with them, hugging and high-fiving when one of the kids made a good play. We were sometimes the only Blazer fans in the stadium. I knew this could be Hal's final game at Valdosta and things would be far less intimate in UK's massive Commonwealth Stadium.

But my press pass was a blessing that afternoon. With chemotherapy scheduled to begin in three days, I had to stay healthy, or else jeopardize the treatments. The sky dumped torrents of rain throughout the chilling afternoon. The press box may have been a zoo, but at least it was warm and dry.

Not so on the field. Unable to move the ball very effectively in the rain-drenched quagmire, Valdosta was eliminated, 24-19. After the game, Hal told his players he was taking the job at Kentucky. They already knew it, but this was the first time they heard it from him. The crushing loss was such a sad way to end such a positive relationship with that team.

Hal's announcement was met with tears, hugs and well-wishing from his players. I got on the team bus twice to say goodbye. I had grown so attached to these young men and their families, and leaving them was difficult and emotional.

Hal had planned on winning the game, so he was scheduled to fly back to Valdosta right after Monday's press conference in Lexington to start preparing for the next round. That would have been great for Valdosta. But the loss was actually Kentucky's gain. It allowed Hal to start recruiting, hire a new staff and begin the rebuilding immediately.

Larry Ivy and two ex-UK players, Talbott Todd and Derrick Ramsey, escorted us to the private jet that had been sent. C.M. and his wife, Evelyn, were expecting us for dinner.

It was dark when we landed in Lexington, so I was deprived a first aerial view of the Bluegrass region's beauty. Larry drove us to C.M.'s house, where we would hide out until Monday's press conference.

Outside, the media frenzy only heightened. The Sunday *Lexington Herald-Leader* continued its speculation, and plastered Hal's picture all over the sports page. C.M. took us on a clandestine tour of the city, and smuggled us into the athletics facilities on campus. I found Lexington to be a lovely town, and was thrilled to be coming here.

On Monday, this well-guarded but widely known secret was to be officially revealed. Media members staked their territory in the press conference room. After the UK Athletics Board officially approved his hiring, Hal was introduced to the press. I couldn't believe how many media people had shoehorned into the room. But they didn't ask any questions of Hal that he hadn't answered before.

At 4 p.m. Hal and I were taken to the Nutter Field House for his first meeting with the Kentucky squad. Again, the media was Hal's shadow. Reporters and cameramen lined the Field House corridors as he made his way to the meeting. But they stopped at the door. Hal had the team all to himself. It was time to start building that magical rapport.

After his introduction, Hal explained his philosophies and outlined his plan to rebuild the Kentucky football program. The young men sat silent and stone-faced. No wonder. As I know well, change is always difficult and the unknown is worse. These players had heard some strange tales about their new coach, about how his practices don't involve the customary all-out contact, about how he doesn't make his players stretch or run.

Hal kept his speech brief and then asked if there were any questions. Still silence. Finally, someone spoke up.

"Coach," he asked, "how are we going to be able to run fast if we don't stretch at practice?"

Hal reached into his bag of tricks and pulled out an icebreaker.

"Have you ever seen a dog stretch before he chases a car?" he replied.

The players roared with laughter. The questions began pouring in. By the end of the session, players were coming up to me to express their excitement to start playing for Hal.

That night we flew back to Valdosta on a private plane provided by one of the UK boosters. There were 64 messages awaiting us on our answering machine, and the phone continued to ring constantly after we arrived. Before addressing any of them, we took time to visit with our children and tell them about the trip.

Hal was going back to Lexington the next day so he packed as many clothes as he could. The next morning Leslie stayed home from school so that she could take her daddy to the airport and say goodbye.

I thought it was only appropriate that the plane taking Hal and assistant coaches Mike Major, Mike Leach and Mike Fanoga to Lexington was painted red and black, the colors of the Valdosta State Blazers.

Afterward I drove Leslie to school, and then continued to Pearlman Cancer Center to begin my chemotherapy. I was terrified, and I knew I wouldn't see my husband again until Christmas Eve.

Hal called often. He was scared, too, and felt like he had abandoned me, even though this is how I wanted it. The phone kept ringing, too. Some members of the media just had to get the story, no matter the cost. One newspaper reporter from Louisville came to Valdosta to write about Hal. I instructed Matt and Karen not to talk to him; I was concerned he might twist their words into a different meaning. Many friends kept me apprised of this reporter's dirt-digging agenda.

Our friend Bill Moore said the writer had become frustrated during their conversation, complaining that "no one had anything bad to say about Hal."

"That's because there isn't anything bad to say about Hal," Bill informed him.

The writer was determined to speak to Matt. Once he learned his phone number, he called Matt's apartment constantly. Matt's roommate took the calls, becoming increasingly tense at the reporter's persistence.

Finally, the roommate cracked. "He's trying to help his mother go through chemotherapy!" he pleaded, hoping to shake the dogged caller.

"His mother has cancer?" the reporter asked.

In an instant, my private story became public. To my surprise, the story about my cancer was written in a positive, compassionate way, which I appreciated and enjoyed. But it didn't make what was ahead of me any easier.

The next day I switched to an unlisted phone number. Anyone who wanted to reach Hal could call Kentucky for information. I needed some peace and quiet to deal with the trials of chemotherapy.

Patty Goss, the mother of Leslie's best friend, began driving me to my chemo sessions and providing the support I desperately needed. A nurse and breast cancer survivor, Patty offered her time and expertise willingly, and coached me through the trying process.

And it was trying. I would go each time with trepidation to the infusion room to receive treatment. It was lined with 15 recliner chairs, each facing a television. There were curtains for privacy and a table and two chairs for patients' use. Ironically, this room that incited such fear looked out into a beautiful atrium; the plants and birds and thriving life helped remind me of what I was fighting for.

I received the chemotherapy drugs intravenously, directly into a vein of my left arm. Since the infection-fighting lymph nodes had been removed from my right arm during my mastectomy, my left arm would have to be used in all future medical procedures as a precaution.

What I mostly feared was the uncertainty. Hal was just as concerned. He called me after my first treatment and asked all kinds of questions to try to ease his concerns. We weren't together physically, but we certainly were going through treatment together.

Chemotherapy drugs work by destroying cells. Treatment is tailored to each patient to make sure the highest dose of medication is used to kill as many cancer cells as possible. The body could not tolerate a single, enormous dose to wipe out all the malignant cells. The higher the risk of recurrence, the more potent and toxic drugs needed. And typically, the higher potency a drug, the worse its side effects.

I was considered at low risk for recurrence, so my treatment would be administered in 12 visits over a six-month period. But no matter how low the risk, the medication was toxic and caused some horrible side effects. My protocol included Zofran, an anti-nausea medication, combined with Decadron, a steroid, followed by Cytoxan, Methorexate and 5-flourouracil or 5-FU.

Cytoxan can cause serious damage to the bladder wall. I was advised to drink plenty of water while it was being administered and for the first 24 hours afterward to flush out the toxic effects.

Methotrexate can cause diarrhea and mouth sores. 5-FU can also cause irritation to the lining of the mouth. To prevent this, I held ice against the inside of my cheeks to reduce the blood flow and limit the amount of medication that reached the lining of my mouth. The ice had to be replaced as it melted.

Each chemotherapy session took about three hours. It felt much longer. My treatment began on a Tuesday, which set the course for the rigid cycle of therapy. It began with two consecutive Tuesdays of blood counts followed by chemotherapy. The third Tuesday I only had blood counts taken to ensure the previous weeks' chemotherapy was not endangering me. The fourth Tuesday was an off day.

Twice, the third Tuesday's blood level check found counts low enough to endanger my health, so I was put on medication. The first time the doctors found my white cell count was low, they feared my immune system would be too weak to fight infection. So

I was placed on antibiotics and restricted to the house to avoid any exposure to illness. My quarantine couldn't have come at a worse time. That same week, Karen caught the flu, became dehydrated and had to go to the hospital. It was her first time in the hospital and she was scared. I wanted so badly to be there with her, but I was under strict orders and couldn't afford to compromise my tenuous health. I couldn't even drive her there.

With Hal in Lexington, Matt had to fill out Karen's admission papers at the hospital. He stayed with her until about 2 a.m. then grabbed a few hours of sleep before his 6 a.m. football workout.

It nearly killed me to have my baby alone in a hospital bed while I sat restricted to my home. I pleaded with my doctor to let me just go stand at the door so we could at least see each other. But it was simply out of the question given my dangerously low white blood cell count.

We all survived that emotional ordeal, but there was much still ahead. I used my off-weeks to rest and gain strength. Twice I visited Hal in Lexington, and another time we went to the beach.

These respites helped me prepare for the next round, but they didn't make the chemotherapy any easier. Each treatment built upon the previous one, causing me to feel more wretched with each passing week. The advancing side effects made it harder and harder to remember how critical it was to do everything possible to attack my cancer. The toxic chemicals invading my body caused hair loss, weight gain, mouth sores, eye problems, nausea, headaches and fatigue. The consuming feeling of misery is impossible to fully describe. I had unwillingly become part of a group that no one wants to join. I knew that, in the best of circumstances, membership meant fear, pain and distress. I also knew that for some, it meant death.

To make matters worse I was forbidden from many of life's little pick-me-ups. I couldn't sit outside and enjoy the beautiful spring weather because exposure to the sun would compromise the drugs used in my treatment. I couldn't receive a manicure because of the risk of infection. Coloring my hair would only accelerate my balding, and that didn't need any help. As predicted, my hair began falling from my head after the first treatments. I noticed it when the floor of the shower was covered with follicles one day. I was sickened. First I had to sacrifice my breast, a part of my body that makes me feel feminine. And now my hair! It didn't all go at once, but it was definitely thinning quickly. I never lost all of my hair, but it was so thin that I usually wore hats or even a wig.

In those trying days, I don't know what I would have done if I hadn't had Hal. My deteriorating appearance didn't bother him at all. When my hair clogged the shower drain that first time, it was Hal who cleaned it up. He just hugged me warmly and told me to go to the other room while he took care of it.

After my surgery, I began filling the right cup of my brassier with a little cotton pillow provided by the organization Reach to Recovery. Because the stuffing was so light, I had to tether the bottom of my bra to my panties to keep the right side from shifting up too high and looking strange.

But by mid-November, my incision had healed well enough that I could be fitted with a prosthesis. Patty Goss had just been through this process, and told me what to expect. The $400 prosthesis was made of silicone and heavy enough to keep a bra weighted down. It also matched the temperature of the rest of the body.

The prosthesis felt reasonably natural, but by the end of the day it would become bulky and uncomfortable. I never thought the day would come when putting on my breast was a part of getting dressed. Emotionally, this became more taxing as time passed.

I came to rely on a group of woman cancer survivors for support and to validate my feelings. As my emotions shifted during each stage of treatment, it helped to talk to those who had already been through what I was experiencing. We all had different stories to share that each woman could draw from.

I also took time to be alone and pray.

Now I have learned that it's okay to have a bad day; it's okay to cry! It is also important to put my disease into perspective and count my blessings. I am married to my best friend, our children are not only doing well in school but they are good people. Our family and friends have been an unending fount of support. When I pray, I thank God for these many blessings.

Fighting cancer is a paradox. While it's an extremely solitary and personal struggle, it also requires an enormous support group. My kids provided a huge dose of this day-to-day support. Matt and Karen handled errands for me, ran the house when I was too weak from chemotherapy treatments, and took great care of their kid sister, Leslie.

My youngest daughter was my greatest motivation to get out of bed each day. No matter how much her older brother and sister were there to pitch in, Leslie needed her mother. I was determined to fulfill this critical role. It kept me going through many tenuous days.

I also relied on our wonderful church, St. John's Catholic. For three months, parishioners and parents from the elementary school prepared meals for me and delivered them to my home.

The kids, the support group and the church all provided sustenance and motivation. But Hal was the key to my recovery. He made countless contributions. But most of all, he listened. That's what I really needed. He would call every morning and night, and in between if I was having a particularly rough day. If I suffered a setback, he would always find the words to help me concentrate on my recovery. He even came back to Valdosta before Kentucky started spring practice, and took me on a lovely vacation at the beach.

Despite all the wonderful support he was giving me, Hal felt helpless. It must be so difficult to watch someone you love cope with this disease. I remember Hal grimacing horribly at one of my regular chemotherapy sessions as he watched a doctor stick me four times before he found a vein. "I thought you're supposed to be here to comfort me, not the other way around," I teased him.

Hal had a lot on his plate. In just four months he had to hire a coaching staff, recruit his first freshman class, evaluate returning talent, prepare for his first spring practice at UK — and worry about me during his absence. Though he tried to hide it, I know how hard it was on him to be away from me during this period. I wasn't looking for any magic words of motivation from Hal; I knew there was no such thing in this fight. I just wanted him to be there for me. And he was.

I will always admire his courage and his ability to tirelessly support me while fulfilling his considerable obligation to the Kentucky football program at the same time.

In February I flew to visit Hal in Lexington for the first time. During that six-month transition period, Hal lived out of a suitcase at the Hyatt Regency. The staff there took good care of him. But we wanted to settle down.

Hal had done some house hunting when he could find a few hours, and we continued the search together in February without luck. But in early April, Hal found the perfect house. He wanted me to see it, but I didn't feel well enough to travel. So I told him to buy it, just as he had told me many years before, in Iowa.

When I felt strong enough to travel later that month, we immediately went to see our new home. Even though Hal had sent me a videotaped tour of the place, he was nervous to show me in person. But his anxiety was foundless. I had loved the video version, and I loved the real thing.

During my weeklong stay, I met with Dr. Ben Roach, founder and chairman of the McDowell Cancer Foundation. Dr. Roach had offered to help me select a team of physicians to continue my care at UK's Markey Cancer Center once I moved to Lexington. He sure knew how to make a person feel special, and I needed that. I wasn't feeling well and was almost ready to quit the chemotherapy. The team he assembled encouraged me to complete my final two treatments. They explained that research suggested the entire course of chemotherapy was necessary to achieve the best results. I asked plenty of questions of this impressive group of doctors, and left the meeting much more optimistic.

I had great confidence in my doctors in Valdosta. But I was also looking forward to benefiting from the expertise offered by the team at the Markey Cancer Center.

Copies of my medical records, slides from surgery and X-ray films were forwarded to the Markey doctors, who agreed with the diagnosis and treatment plan I was on. I was reassured we had made the right choices.

They were also willing to let me participate fully in my recovery, a decision I had made early on. I looked at my physicians as the coaches and myself as the player. They drew up the game plan and I would follow their instructions to get the win.

My recovery plan included exercise and diet. Important for an athlete who wants to get ahead, a healthy diet and exercise regimen was vital for my survival. I worked out with a personal trainer twice a week in Valdosta and walked three miles a day. I met with a nutritionist to help me get the most out of every meal. I was determined to stay physically strong to combat the withering side effects of chemotherapy.

My spiritual strength came from God. Several times a day, I recited a prayer my mother taught me to say each morning before I went to school. The prayer invoked my guardian angel to take care of me. On particularly rough days, I would even ask if he could solicit the help of any angel friends who weren't too busy to join him in my care.

Friends and strangers alike in Kentucky, Georgia, Texas and Iowa included me in their prayers.

Everyone has his or her own bag of troubles. Given the choice, I would still pick mine. I'm blessed to be in a position where I can concentrate on my recovery and raise money and awareness for cancer prevention. I have come to believe that God is using me as a messenger to educate people, and help them understand how cancer impacts not only the patient's life, but also the lives around her. It is a personal disease and it is a community disease.

And it isn't going away. Cancer continues to take the lives of too many people we care about. No amount of treatment, attitude, exercise, nutrition and faith can save everyone. NBC-TV recently reported that one of every four deaths in America is caused by cancer. By the year 2003, cancer will be the leading cause of death in America.

This year 182,000 women will be diagnosed with breast cancer, including 2,400 in Kentucky, and 44,000 women who already have breast cancer will die from the disease.

During the 1997-98 basketball season the finality of cancer's clutches hit close to home. That spring Allen Edwards, a senior on UK's basketball team, lost his mother to the merciless disease. This terrified me. I wondered if the cancer would invade me again. Unfortunately, no one can tell what the future holds. No survivor's clean bill of health is guaranteed.

The frightening reminders continue to surround me. I know two people who have died of cancer since my diagnosis and I have two friends who are struggling to survive cancer that has spread from its original site.

After my week in Kentucky, I returned to Valdosta to sell our house and complete preparations for the move at the end of May. It was time. Time to finish my two remaining chemotherapy treatments. Time to begin our much-anticipated new life in Kentucky.

Sometimes life has a sick sense of irony. Our greatest opportunity — the head football coaching job at UK — came at the same time that we faced our greatest challenge. Both required massive amounts of courage, persistence and luck. But it's amazing what we can accomplish when we make up our minds.

Like Hal's aggressive credo says, "When surrounded by superior forces, attack, attack, attack!"

4th and Goal — Great Expectations

"Never take counsel of your fears!"
— T.J. Jackson, a favorite quote of Hal Mumme

I t's not enough to want to succeed — you must put yourself in position to achieve your goal! The University of Kentucky has put itself in a position to win with a real commitment to the football program. It has built state-of-the-art facilities, funded the program appropriately, provided scholastic support to players through the tutorial program and hired the best people to run the athletic administration.

It's fourth and goal! UK has done its job. Now, it's Hal's turn to score, in league with his coaching staff and student athletes.

UK offered us the job of our dreams. And we plan to make the most of it. In just one year, our entire family has already become deeply attached to Kentucky — the state, the people and the University.

We are extremely grateful to Dr. Charles Wethington, C.M. Newton and the UK Athletics Association for giving us this rare opportunity. It took great courage and vision for them to make so radical a choice for such an important position. And we can't thank the Big Blue fans enough for their warm welcome to the Bluegrass. We weren't surprised to hear the skepticism when Hal was picked to turn around the Kentucky program. Hal who? Valdosta where? Of course we heard those comments. Wildcat fans would have been crazy not to say them. But after the initial shock, I found that most Kentuckians understood the reasoning behind Hal's hire.

I was overwhelmed by the mountains of cards and letters that came from UK fans in every corner of the state and beyond, wishing me well and praying for me as I battled my breast cancer. I kept every card and will treasure them forever.

A Kentucky fan living in Valdosta sent one of my favorites shortly after Hal was named head coach at UK in the first week of December. We didn't know Debbie and Ken Bruce when we lived in Georgia, but I passed their house every day when I drove Leslie to school. I wondered who owned that Kentucky flag that flew every time the Wildcats were playing on the gridiron or the hardwood. Debbie's card read: "Thank you, thank you, thank you. Who says there's no such thing as Santa Claus? Santa came early for us UK fans."

This kind of enthusiasm and support meant the world as we prepared to make our giant leap to the big leagues.

We packed up and arrived in Lexington June 1. While we awaited our furniture, Hal and I stayed at the Hilton Suites. There the staff welcomed us with a room-full of blue and white balloons, pom pons and other UK memorabilia, as well as a luscious fruit and dessert tray. What a great first impression. I felt so welcomed and special.

Our son, Matt, had decided to transfer to Kentucky and continue playing for his father, even though this meant he'd have to forfeit one of his two remaining years of eligibility. Through Matt's experiences as player, I learned so much about Hal. Before we met, I had no concept of football, so I assumed all coaches taught and treated players the way he does. Matt's devotion to Hal, as a player, opened my eyes to just how special a gift my husband brought to a team.

Hal teaches young men much more than how to position their bodies on the field. He's not a coach who needs the perfect specimen at every position, or who manipulates players like chess pieces to implement his strategy. Instead, he prefers to develop players, to coax out the best in each and every one. He builds from the ground up, instilling an understanding of strategy, fostering an ability to think on their feet.

Many coaches have subscribed to the time-honored survival-of-the-fittest philosophy, in which the best players are the ones still standing at the end of a tortuous practice session or bloody game. This is not Hal's way. His methods are unconventional, but to good purpose. Practices last less than two hours to keep players' minds fresh to process and retain complex information. Limited contact in practice ensures players will be healthy, strong and hungry come game day. The quarterback is always off-limits to tacklers to minimize the chances of injury at this critical position. And Hal stays positive, choosing to build his players' confidence with affirmation rather than to scare them with threats and verbal attacks.

What mother would not want her son to play for this kind of coach and have this kind of an athletic experience? I was thrilled Matt had decided to follow his dad, and I'll be even more thrilled when he finally dons the Blue and White this fall, his final season of eligibility.

Karen had her own athletic — not to mention personal — life at Valdosta State. She decided to remain in Georgia with the understanding that we would fly her to Lexington almost monthly.

Our high-schooler, Leslie, negotiated an extra 10 days in Valdosta as part of her lucrative moving agreement with her daddy.

The package included not only the extra time with friends in Georgia, but also a guitar and lessons, a dog and the promise of no more Catholic school. Hal was so easy.

I was not. I put my foot down at the school request. A Catholic education was non-negotiable. I believed the discipline and curriculum a Catholic school offered were too valuable to give up for a daughter's whim. And the dog we bought Leslie wasn't exactly what she had in mind. The black-and-white cocker spaniel figurine now sits proudly on her desk, where it never barks, gets hungry, sheds hair or makes a mess — it's a family joke. I'm no fool. Leslie is the first to admit she is far too social to take on a living, breathing responsibility. I knew who really would have taken care of a dog in our household — me. Thank goodness I overruled Hal.

At least Leslie got her guitar. She played it for a while before having it autographed by a host of celebrities at the John Michael Montgomery Golf Tournament. Then she presented it to her brother on his birthday. A country music fan through and through, Matt cherishes the gift, almost as much as he cherishes the giver.

Hal wants every little boy in Kentucky to dream about playing football for the Wildcats. To help accomplish this goal, he set out early and often to gather grassroots support. Great fan support translates to positive feelings about the program, and that encourages the top players in the state to stay home and enjoy the best collegiate playing experience possible. So, long before I was able to join him in Lexington, Hal had hit the road to meet the fans in every corner of the state. He appreciates his warm reception by those countless Big Blue partisans.

The day after the moving company unloaded our furniture and belongings, I accompanied Hal, Assistant Alumni Director Stan Key and Associate Athletics Director Kathy DeBoer on a whistle-stop tour of Bowling Green, Cadiz and Paducah. At a lovely reception at Bowling Green's Corvette Museum, I met an 80-year-old Wildcat fan who bent my ear with lively tales of the offspring she cared to claim

— that is, the ones who graduated from Kentucky. She added that her family took her to UK's first home game every year to celebrate her birthday. This was a real fan. And she said she had wanted to meet me, not Hal. She wanted to know the woman behind the man who coached her beloved UK football team. I was flattered.

The Paducah reception was different, and potentially uncomfortable. One of Hal's first decisions as head coach was to promote Tim Couch to starting quarterback. Tim's rifle arm and amazing field vision are the kind of skills upon which dynasties are built. But this was Billy Jack Haskins country, his hometown. UK's beloved blue-collar leader had decided to transfer rather than move to another position for his senior year. One of his relatives wasted no time in questioning Hal's demotion of the town's favorite son. But Hal defused the volatile situation with a calm, detailed explanation of the situation. I was proud of him for his adept handling of a fragile predicament.

As I hustled through a busy summer in our new home, fatigue and fear were my biggest challenges. Our life had taken an exciting turn and I really wanted to feel well enough to enjoy the ride. But the slowness of my recovery and my increased need for rest were dragging me down. Between alumni events, our new house, the children and Hal, I found it difficult to accomplish as much as I had hoped in those first months in Kentucky. I felt like there was so much more I should be doing. After all, I was a mom, the heartbeat of the family! I was the one who set our pace. And now my pace was creeping.

Hal encouraged me to stop worrying about everyone else, and take care of myself first. He suggested I get help with the house and learn to delegate some of the work. It was good advice. I've always lived an active life and have tried to be everything to everyone. But I knew if I didn't get healthy, I wouldn't be anything to anyone. So I am learning I don't have to do it all.

Through this unexpectedly tiring stage of my recovery, Hal was

117

my rock. He provided the patience and inspiration I desperately needed. While I prepared Leslie for school each weekday morning, Hal would sit at a little table in our bedroom, selecting Bible verses for me, and writing daily notes of encouragement. After he and Leslie left, I would retreat to our room, anxious to read the day's message and verse. I knew that God would show me the way to conquer the disease, and my fear. It also helped that our favorite priest, Father Lou Schmidt at Mary Queen of the Holy Rosary, always seemed to have the perfect message for us at Sunday mass.

I needed all the help I could get. Cancer is a silent disease. With no way to know whether I had any malignant cells remaining in my body, fear became a daily companion. But I am a strong, determined woman. I would pray and remember Hal's words to his teams: "Never take counsel of your fears!" It's good advice for everyone, but difficult to follow.

Fear creates an elevated level of cautiousness. A common cold or bit of congestion triggers irrational worries that new tumors are growing in the lungs. Achy joints can feel like the onset of bone cancer. Many cancer survivors have assured me this experience is common.

When breast cancer does spread, it most commonly invades the tissues of the lungs, liver and bones. The greatest possibility of recurrence takes place during the first two years. But there's never a guarantee; you're never in the clear. And that's scary.

I've learned that cancer patients who have completed surgery and chemotherapy are called one of two things: a survivor or in remission. Before I had the disease, I thought a cancer survivor was a person who had cancer, received treatment and had been cured. Now I know that's not exactly correct.

I realize I haven't been cured; my cancer is in remission. This more accurate term to describe my experience doesn't infer a conclusion.

But I'm doing great! The tumor is gone, but cancer will always be a part of my life. Learning to overcome the fear of a recurrence is paramount to my continuing recovery. Because the process is continuing. After my aggressive surgery and chemo treatments were completed, I began hormone therapy. Since my tumor was estrogen-receptor positive, hormone therapy offered additional protection in the event of a recurrence.

This stage of my treatment included taking a drug called Tamoxifen twice a day for five years. After being monitored weekly for six months, I would now cut back to a visit every three months.

On the fourth of July, I received a reminder just how uncertain "recovery" can be. My friend from Valdosta, Patty Goss, called. Her cancer was back. It had metastasized and she had 10 tumors on her lungs. Patty was 42 years old at the time of her original diagnosis. Like me, she had suffered no lymph node involvement.

Her call terrified me. I am very concerned for Patty and her family. The news once again reminded just how insidious cancer is. There isn't even a test to detect a recurrence until the tumor appears.

Patty and her husband traveled to Duke University Medical Center seeking help. She would have to begin another round of chemotherapy. This time her drug protocol included Taxol and Adriamycin, and the side effects were difficult to endure.

When her body did not respond to the powerful drugs, the doctors tried a third treatment plan. This time the tumors responded, and Patty was admitted to the Duke hospital for a stem-cell transplant, a procedure that removes and stores the patient's own bone marrow and stem cells. Then the patient is sedated for days while the most powerful chemotherapy drugs available are administered under constant supervision. Finally the stockpiled bone marrow and stem cells are replaced inside the patient.

Stem-cell transplantation costs about $100,000, and is used only in advanced cases. Some insurance companies resist paying for this risky procedure. As of this writing, Patty doesn't know whether the transplant has increased her chances of survival. She told me she has a one-in-four chance the procedure was successful.

Rita Munn, my oncologist, and Pat McGrath, my general surgeon, tried to reassure me and help me through this rough time. But how could I forget about the dangers? Cancer is a minefield. As I dressed and undressed each day, my body was — and is — a vivid reminder.

Hal's work schedule became more demanding in early August when the players arrived for preseason practice. Every night Hal would update me on the team's progress.

Our son, Matt, wasn't eligible to play in games that first season because he had transferred. But he could practice, and make a significant contribution. The other players peppered him with questions about Hal and the new system. Tim Couch, in particular, picked Matt's brain for pointers about the complex offense.

The entire state was buzzing about the coming season. There was so much anticipation, shared by both the fans and the media. Hal Mumme masks began to pop up everywhere. I learned that Kentucky fans love to tell stories. I loved each one I heard.

Hal's debut came August 30 against cross-state rival Louisville. The Cardinals had beaten the Cats two straight years, and felt they had good cause to be confident. Louisville fans even boasted that the street — Cooper Drive — next to UK's Commonwealth Stadium was named in honor of their coach, Ron Cooper. Lexington Mayor Pam Miller evened the score by renaming a stretch of Cooper Drive, "Hal Mumme Pass."

That my husband had opening day jitters was no wonder. This was the biggest opening day of our lives. Hal wasn't sure what to expect from his new team. And we both knew how high the stakes were. This was more than just a rivalry. This game would set the tone for Hal's career at Kentucky.

Nervous as I was, I managed to thoroughly enjoy the pregame pageantry. The UK marching band delivered a spirited warmup concert. The fan-fueled rendition of "My Old Kentucky Home," was incredibly moving. But it struck the final note of buildup. It was show time. I don't show much emotion at a game, knowing that people are watching me closely. But inside, I'm a tangle of emotion. My stomach was in knots as Hal's first Wildcat squad took the field. The setting was different, the magnitude far greater than anything we'd seen.

But some things were the same. I had watched Hal run the offense at Iowa Wesleyan and Valdosta State to great success. Now it was Tim Couch's turn to execute Hal's passing attack. He and the unheralded receiver corps clicked immediately. After the first touchdown I relaxed a bit. And after the Cats trounced the Cards, 38-24, I was on top of the world.

I've always enjoyed watching Hal interact with his team on the sideline. His behavior was no less fascinating in this first game at Kentucky. The setting was vastly different, from the carnival atmosphere to the throngs of fans to the massive press corps. But Hal's routine was the same. When the offense isn't on the field, he brings the quarterbacks, receivers and running backs together briefly to make adjustments and plan the next offensive series. Meanwhile, Mike Major has complete control of the defensive unit at work; Hal sometimes only sees defensive play when he watches the film the next day.

Hal's success has always sprung from his ability to focus on the present, and inspire his teams to do the same. "Play the next play" is one of his favorite expressions. He instills the importance of letting bygones be bygones. Whether the previous down was a score or a turnover, the most important play is always the next one.

By recognizing the impossibility of changing the past, Hal puts all of his energy into something he does have a say in — the future. He often reminds his players the past does not predict the future, which was great advice for me, too, as I tried to conquer my ominous enemy, cancer. During treatment, I often drew from Hal's wisdom, and always tried to "play the next play."

After a 35-27 loss at Mississippi State, Kentucky headed to Indiana to play the Hoosiers, a team Hal felt UK should beat. I had made a habit of traveling with the team to every game, whether by bus or plane. I liked being with my husband on trips and, according to long-time team trainer Jim Madaleno, so did Hal. Jim claimed his boss was calmer when I came along.

But this wasn't the case at Indiana. Hal's nervousness was painfully obvious, even before the team left Lexington. He has always been more nervous playing games he felt his team should win; he's incredibly calm against an opponent like Florida or Tennessee.

Before departing, the team sat down for dinner together at the Hilton Suites. Hal had told his players to wear their nylon warmup suits, but some showed up in shorts and T-shirts. He was angry. To make matters worse, the bus trip to Bloomington dragged on much longer than anticipated.

Hal's testiness only worsened on game day. When he arrived for breakfast in a T-shirt and shorts, I whispered to Mike Major, loud enough for Hal to hear, "I don't think Hal's attire is appropriate."

He didn't think my comment was funny. He was in no mood for teasing.

I usually watch the pre-game motivational video with the team. But after my poorly received ribbing about his casual outfit, I thought it best to leave him alone.

Hal's annoyance with me turned out to be just the tip of the iceberg. His mood affected everyone on the team. When he didn't feel he had 100 percent of each player's attention after the video, he hurled a table across the room, shattering the unlucky piece of furniture upon landing. Suffice it to say that this was a rare outburst. Hal doesn't lose his temper often and my guess is that he threw the table more for effect than out of rage. He wanted to startle them back to the reality of the day, and get them mentally ready to play.

Whatever the reason, the pre-game explosion worked. Tim Couch launched seven touchdown passes, including four caught by Craig Yeast, and Kentucky rolled to an impressive 49-7 victory.

At halftime I met Indiana basketball coach Bob Knight, notorious for once throwing a chair across the hardwood during a game. The living legend complimented Hal after watching the first-half massacre of his school's football team. I thanked him and said I had been thinking about him that morning.

Confused, he asked, "When were you thinking about me this morning?"

"Right after Hal threw the table," I said, thinking again about the infamous incident.

I wasn't sure what to expect from Knight. After a moment he looked at me, began laughing and said, "I think I'm going to like you."

I certainly liked the game. Hal was able to take Couch out of the game after the third quarter and let backup Dusty Bonner log some playing time. This was an important victory, a great confidence-builder.

The eye-catching win also boosted natural interest in this high-flying new brand of Kentucky football. CBS decided to televise the Wildcats' next game, versus mighty Florida. This rated as one Hal did not expect to win. The Gators came into the tilt ranked No. 1 in the country. The Kentucky players looked nervous and, sure enough, they suffered a disastrous start. Florida jumped on early Wildcat miscues to take a quick 28-0 lead in the first quarter.

I had agreed to do a live sideline interview about my battle with breast cancer during the second quarter. But after the lop-sided start, CBS decided to put the interview on hold, and I was grateful. They did tell our story in the fourth quarter, but I was not interviewed.

Hal and his team didn't quit after the devastating start. In the second quarter UK was pinned on fourth down deep in its own territory, and lined up to punt. Ever the gambler, Hal called a fake punt play. It worked to perfection. Blocker A.J. Simon's completion to James Whalen caught the Gators, the fans and the

CBS crew off guard.

Who would try such a dangerous sneak attack? Kentucky fans were thrilled by Hal's aggressive play calling. Even Florida coach Steve Spurrier, another well-documented risk-taker, loved the brash move. He loves to share the story at conventions and meetings.

The clandestine play led to a touchdown and an enormous momentum shift. Like a shot of confidence, the fake punt emboldened the Wildcats to match Florida down-for-down the rest of the way. Kentucky took 28 points from the vaunted Florida defense.

Moreover, Kentucky's stand against the nation's top team emboldened Hal's squad for a better day just ahead. The very next week, Alabama came to town. Kentucky hadn't beaten the Crimson Tide for 75 years. I thought of 98-year-old Turner Gregg, the quarterback who led the last Kentucky squad to top Alabama in 1922. I had read in the newspaper that Turner's remaining goals were to live to 100, and to see UK beat Alabama again. But he was running out of time. After this game, Alabama would be off UK's schedule until 2005.

Fans were so excited about the game. Despite the long odds, people seemed to expect the upset.

Karen flew in from Georgia to watch the game. Hal's parents and brother, Jeff, flew in from Texas. In all the years Hal had coached, they had seen only a handful of games. That evening they witnessed a classic.

After 60 thrilling minutes, the score was deadlocked at 34. Exactly one year ago, Hal's Valdosta State team had toppled nemesis North Alabama in triple overtime. Now Kentucky did the same to 'Bama, only this time it just took one overtime to get the job done.

The final was 40-34. What a victory! The overflow crowd went wild. Hordes of fans stampeded onto the field to celebrate and congratulate the Wildcat players. Hal's parents and my children wanted to descend on the field, too, but I cautioned them not to leave our booth until the fans calmed down. Even at Valdosta, it was wise to give a rowdy crowd time to settle after a big win.

From our lofty perch in the press box, we watched the goal posts joyfully toppled in victory. I never could have imagined so fantastic a site. As I walked about the stadium, I watched grown men cry. It was a great and emotional moment.

At Copperas Cove, Iowa Wesleyan and Valdosta State, I had always joined Hal on the field after he finished talking to the team. At Valdosta we began walking together to his post-game radio show. This was impossible at Kentucky, especially after a monumental win like this one. By the time I reached the press conference room, Hal was already answering questions. When he saw my face, he winked. That wink has replaced our post-game walk.

Traffic was a mess after the game, but a wonderful mess, the kind that's more dream than nightmare. It was as if no one wanted to leave the stadium parking lot. Everyone was having too much fun.

Over the years Hal and I have established a comfortable post-game routine. After the frenzy of game day, we retreat to the sanctuary of our home. When we finally made it home that night, we were greeted by an answering machine full of messages from well-wishers. Many thought we weren't answering the phone, but really we were just stuck in the happy traffic jam.

According to habit, Hal usually retires to the family room and reviews statistics or watches a game on TV. You couldn't tell whether we won or lost by watching him. This game was no different. Though we stayed up until 3 a.m. watching the replay of the game, Hal viewed it with the scrutinizing eye of a coach.

It's no wonder Leslie thinks her Daddy's football games are boring. She lives in her own separate universe. If she can possibly find something to do with her friends, she'd rather not go to the game. Afterward, she rarely even asks about the outcome. When she was in grade school, Leslie challenged Hal one Thursday night, five days after the last contest. "Daddy, why didn't you tell me you won the football game?" she asked.

125

"Because you didn't ask," Hal replied with a knowing, fatherly grin.

We've always encouraged our children to pursue their own interests and foster their own lives away from football and us. The game was their daddy's livelihood, but we didn't want his career to dictate their lives.

The Alabama victory sent Hal's stock at Kentucky soaring. The following week, C.M. Newton informed us he was already working on a new contract for Hal. Fans were more supportive than ever. Several times during that first season, C.M. received a barely legible note from a dedicated UK booster with a $10 bill attached "to take care of the new coach." I couldn't make out the name, and the envelope had no return address. We would love to meet that fan or at least send him a thank you.

The Wildcats were 3-2 heading into the South Carolina game October 11. This was a particularly emotional week for me; it was the first anniversary of my diagnosis of breast cancer.

Kentucky lost on the road, 38-24. Hal took the setback hard; he didn't feel the team had played its best. But the game didn't shake C.M.'s confidence in his new coach. On the flight back from South Carolina, C.M. took out a legal pad, wrote down the key points of Hal's new contract, ripped off the page and passed it up to Hal for our perusal. I laughed and told C.M. about the time Hal learned about his salary at Copperas Cove in the same unceremonious way. Hal said all great minds think alike.

The extension was a pleasant surprise and a boost for recruiting. We didn't know how long C.M. would even be staying on as UK's athletics director, but it was so nice to know we could count on someone's word. It was wonderful doing business this way. There were no hidden agendas. Hal wanted the extension because of recruiting, not money. He still doesn't concern himself with financial matters. It was more important to him that high school seniors knew he would be around for their entire collegiate careers.

The homecoming game against Northeast Louisiana marked another emotional milestone for me. It was October 18, the first anniversary of my mastectomy. The morning of the game the McDowell Cancer Foundation sponsored a brunch and fashion show at Andover Country Club to celebrate life and survival after breast cancer. I served as one of the models in the show, and took the opportunity to share my story.

Hal was restless all day; kickoff was not until later that evening. He thought Kentucky should win the game, but knew Northeast Louisiana would be no pushover. The Indians had beaten UK the last time they played, and tested Georgia earlier in the season. But his anxiety was unfounded. The Cats were commanding and won 49-14.

The following week, in a Georgia downpour, Kentucky had its chances but wound up on the losing end of the 23-13 final. I knew Hal would be disappointed and wanted to be with him after the game. But I didn't have access to the post-game press area. Luckily, Kathy DeBoer came to the rescue.

The assistant AD took me by the arm and escorted me through various checkpoints. "I've got Hal Mumme's wife," she told the stadium staff as we sped toward the press area. When we arrived I knew something wasn't right. By now I recognized most of UK's large media entourage. But none of these faces looked familiar. We were in the Georgia press room, decked out in Kentucky blue! Everyone was staring. But before I had a chance to get embarrassed, Kathy grabbed my arm again and whisked me to safety.

After that misadventure I was glad to be back in a friendly stadium the next week. We were playing LSU, and I stopped by the visitor's booth in the Commonwealth Stadium press box to introduce myself to the schools athletics department representatives and the opposing head coach's wife. I chatted with the wife of Tigers coach Gerry DiNardo, and shared some old LSU stories with AD Joe Dean. I also met some representatives from the Sugar

Bowl who had come to scout the explosive Bayou Bengals. I jumped on the chance to do a little promoting of our own explosive team. When I saw there weren't enough chairs in the LSU booth for everyone, I invited the Sugar Bowl reps to sit with me. They refused politely. But as I was leaving, I told them, "Don't forget to invite us to the Sugar Bowl some day. They'll have to shut down the state of Kentucky because we'll all be in New Orleans!"

It can happen, too.

Kentucky lost that game to LSU, 63-28, then beat Vanderbilt, 21-10, to level its record at 5-5 heading into the season's finale against Tennessee. As was my tradition, before the game I went to introduce myself to Vicky Fulmer, the wife of UT coach Phillip Fulmer. She wasn't in the booth so I left a message that I'd come back later.

When I returned to the Kentucky booth I started to tell a Tennessee joke to my guests, UK fans all. "What do you call a beautiful woman on the arm of a Tennessee graduate?" I asked.

Before I could deliver the punch line, I looked up and saw Vicky at the door. I was mortified. But she didn't appear to have heard the beginning of my off-color joke, or if she had, she wasn't letting on. Convinced I had averted an embarrassing situation, I regained my composure and we had a nice visit. Vicky said she usually didn't get to meet the opposing coach's wife. She was really sweet and gracious.

The game was a regular shootout, with Tennessee getting the better of the 59-31 score. It was a great game for both teams, and the fans certainly got their money's worth. Afterward, I found Vicky again and congratulated her. Later she wrote me a note complimenting Hal on the great job he had done his first year. She confided he made her husband nervous.

I was so glad Vicky hadn't heard my joke. I didn't mean to be personal, just funny. I have learned to be more careful.

But not too careful to reveal the answer to my interrupted question: What do you call a beautiful woman on the arm of a Tennessee graduate? A tattoo, of course.

After the game, we went out with Bill Samuels of Maker's Mark. Bill presented us a framed, autographed print of a special-edition Maker's bottle wrapped up like a mummy, along with a real thing enclosed in a tomb. We proudly display this conversation piece in our home.

The loss to Tennessee left Kentucky a game short of a winning record. But it was quite a season, a success by anyone's measure. The Wildcats broke or tied 51 school records, 15 Southeastern Conference marks, and one NCAA record. Tim Couch completed 363 of 547 passes for 3,884 yards, and broke or tied 17 school and 10 SEC bests by himself. His 37 touchdown passes was the most ever in the NCAA by a sophomore. Craig Yeast led the league in receiving with 73 catches for 873 yards. Hal's high-flying offense performed beyond expectations; the Cats averaged 474 yards and 31.6 points per game. And the first-year coach was named GTE Region II Coach of the Year in a vote of his peers. The fans seemed more than satisfied; every game was a sellout. Just as he had accomplished at every level of his coaching, Hal had instilled the belief that UK could score any down and win every week.

I enjoyed every minute of the season, taking care of my family and becoming involved in our new community. Because of my breast cancer, I had many requests to speak and make appearances at a variety of fund-raising events. Janetta Owens, Hal's administrative assistant, was incredibly helpful with scheduling because most of the speaking requests came through the football office.

But I wasn't myself. Sometimes I think I have only two speeds — stop and go! I honored as many requests as I could; I wanted to make a contribution. My professional goal had been to run my own health care marketing business. But that goal has changed. Now I want to educate people about cancer and raise funds to help researchers develop better treatments and, someday, a cure.

I devote much of my time to the McDowell Cancer Foundation, which raises money for facilities, equipment and research at UK's

Markey Cancer Center. All of the funds we raise support cancer researchers and patients in Kentucky. This is important to us.

As for my bout with cancer, I still undergo regular follow-up care. Oncologist Rita Munn and Pat McGrath, director of the Comprehensive Breast Care Center at UK, take care of me now. If I had a recurrence, Hal and I would rely on these two able physicians for advice.

I have been impressed with UK's Comprehensive Center, which truly lives up to its name. It offers everything necessary: state-of-the-art diagnostic equipment and the physicians and staff to detect, diagnose and treat breast cancer at every stage. When I was diagnosed, I had to go to one facility for my mammogram, another for the physical exam, another to consult with a surgeon, and yet another to meet with an oncologist. Four trips to four different offices in four days!

My battle with cancer wasn't finished when the tumor was destroyed. The experience had left me gaping physical and emotional scars as well. While Hal was busy with his first season, I scheduled an appointment with Dr. Henry Vasconez, chief of plastic surgery at UK, and Dr. Ken Foon, director of the Markey Cancer Center, to discuss my taking an experimental breast cancer vaccine, and the possibility of reconstructing my right breast.

Fear was not going to get the best of me. I wanted to make plans for the future. Meeting with the pair of experts was my first step toward getting on with my life.

There is no commercially available vaccine for breast cancer. But there are experimental vaccines in the works. At the Markey Center, Dr. Foon and Dr. Malaya Chatterjee had been working to develop cancer vaccines for 12 years. Most of their work focused on colon cancer. But in 1992, the two introduced an experimental breast cancer vaccine that uses "anti-idiotype antibodies." Cancer is an invader that, for unknown reasons, the immune system doesn't recognize. Drs. Foon and Chatterjee found that these anti-idiotype antibodies mimic a specific protein on the tumor cells that helps a patient's immune system recognize and destroy the cancer cells.

I was eligible, and willing, to participate in a clinical study for this vaccine. I planned to begin immediately and put off breast reconstruction surgery until June. This would be a much better time for Hal and Leslie to deal with a post-surgery me.

In November, I began the two-year breast cancer vaccine study. The first two months, I received an injection every two weeks. After that, the injections are monthly through November 1999.

I am participating in this study for several reasons. First, I want to do everything possible to avoid a recurrence. Second, it demands I be monitored monthly, which means any recurrence should be detected earlier. And third, because I have two daughters, I want to help find new treatments to protect them from the agony of breast cancer.

There are no medical reasons to go through breast reconstruction surgery. It is an elective procedure that can be done at the time of the mastectomy or years later. My surgeon in Valdosta had encouraged me to consider reconstruction to help me forget the pain and fear. He told me I was too young to have to live like this.

I decided I needed the surgery, both physically and mentally. My prosthesis was terribly cumbersome and unnatural feeling. At night, I held a pillow on the right side of my chest to relieve the discomfort. I also hoped the reconstruction would help me move on — I'll never forget. Never.

I told Dr. Vasconez I better proceed with the reconstruction surgery or else seek professional help. I was dressing and undressing in the closet, hiding my body from my own husband. I didn't want to see myself and avoided looking in mirrors. Women who have had this same experience assured me I'm in good company. What a relief it was to know I wasn't going crazy after all!

Through it all, Hal continued to think of me as the girl in the red bathing suit he met so long ago at Ponderosa Pines swim club. He would be comfortable with whatever decision I made, but it was difficult for him to watch me struggling to cope with my body.

Dr. Vasconez explained a few things about men in Hal's position. He said that most husbands are very supportive of whatever their wives decide. But once the decision to have reconstruction surgery has been made, they have definite opinions about how they'd like the new breast to look. Size seems to be the most popular request. I already had plenty of size, so youthful appearance was my goal. This got no resistance from Hal. I was thrilled, too. It was a rare opportunity to turn back the clock.

I learned there are several options for reconstruction surgery. The simplest places a balloon-like expander beneath the chest muscle. The expander is inflated every few weeks with a saline solution, before a permanent implant is inserted three to six months later. This option offers the quickest recovery. I had spoken to several women who were happy with the results of their expander procedure. But Dr. Vasconez didn't think I was a good candidate for this option because so much tissue had been removed during my mastectomy. And the hollow area beneath my collarbone would also have to be reconstructed.

My doctor recommended I go with a more-complicated free flap procedure, in which tissue from the tummy, buttock or back is removed and transferred to the chest, where it is then sculptured into a breast. This is also the lengthiest and most precise of the available reconstruction procedures because hair-thin blood vessels in the tissue must be severed then reattached through microsurgery. The reforming of the nipple and areola is done at a later date. The option would also mean a longer recovery, but the results would be very natural looking.

We decided to use tissue from my abdomen. Because there wasn't enough tissue available to duplicate the left breast, I agreed to have that breast reduced to achieve symmetry. Since I was undergoing the most complicated option, I wanted to use only my own tissue to recreate my breast. I didn't want to use an implant just to achieve size.

When I first met with Dr. Vasconez in October, I had decided to put off surgery until summer for all the wrong reasons. I thought about everyone but me. Thanksgiving weekend Hal sat me down and told me to make my decision based on what was right for me, not him, recruiting, spring practice or Leslie.

"We'll work around you," he promised.

I didn't want to wait until June. The next week I went to see Dr. Vasconez. We scheduled surgery for January 21. Yes, Leslie would be in school. And yes, Hal would be in the thick of recruiting season. But I desperately wanted to get on with my life. If I could finish my recovery well before the 1998 football season began, that would be a bonus.

Though I had countless preparations to make before the surgery, I didn't let them get in the way of my excitement. I was told I wouldn't be able lift anything heavier than a milk jug for six weeks after the surgery, so I had to make arrangements for the care of Leslie and our house. I donated four units of blood to be used during my surgery in case I needed a transfusion. Dr. Vasconez would need all four units.

On January 21 we arrived at the UK Medical Center at 6 a.m. Ben and Linda Roach sat with us at the hospital until I was called to the pre-surgery room. Hal stayed with me until they wheeled me to the operating room. Sherry Stickel, one of the medical technicians from the Markey Cancer Center, came to see me before I went into surgery. She tied a blue and white ribbon around my ankle and explained it was a good-luck ribbon that came from a corsage she had been given when the UK basketball team won the national championship in 1996.

My highly recommended anesthesiologist, Dr. Richard Lock, tried to start an IV before the surgery. But after two unsuccessful attempts he decided to wait until we were in the operating room. Sensing I was nervous, Dr. Lock asked if I wanted something to help my anxiety. I accepted gladly. The drug he gave me made me feel wonderful. I have no memory of what I said after that. Hal later informed me that I gave away enough football tickets to fill an entire end zone at Commonwealth Stadium.

The surgery was supposed to take six or seven hours. It took 10. The blood vessels in my chest were small and in poor condition, so the microsurgery was more difficult than expected. Hal said the doctor looked like he had played a football game by the time the surgery was finished.

Hal went to the football office while I was in surgery. Dr. Vasconez's assistant called every hour with progress reports. The waiting must have been excruciating. The final call, telling him the surgery was complete, didn't come until 9 p.m.

After three hours in the recovery room, I was transferred to the intensive care burn unit. Hal stayed until 2 a.m. We had anticipated a 24-hour stay in the ICBU, but it turned into a four-day ordeal. The success of the procedure depends on how well the blood supply to the transplanted tissue is re-established. Because the surgery took so long, fluid accumulated in my lungs and pneumonia became a major concern. And the tissue transplant had to be monitored constantly for rejections.

At least that's what I was told. I remember little of those days, except that it was difficult to breath and even harder to speak. I received oxygen and was asked to perform painful breathing exercises. I really didn't want to follow the therapist's instructions, and Hal knew it. So he told the respiratory staff to cut me no slack.

I tried to follow the nurses' instructions, but kept falling asleep. Heather Byrne, my favorite nurse, was attentive and tough. She told me to leave the oxygen mask on my face at all times. When I took it off and fell asleep once, causing my lips to turn blue, she chastised me for failing to follow her orders.

The other thing I vividly recall is being hot. The room temperature was set at a balmy 90 degrees. This helped prevent my blood vessels from constricting in the transplanted tissue. No matter how much I begged for relief from the heat, the staff would not give in. The warm environment gave the tissue its best chance to thrive. In my heat-induced dementia, Hal and the others would occasionally trick me into thinking they had turned down the thermostat, when in fact they were just pretending.

Hal sat in that steam room for four long days, his clothes as soaked with sweat as if he had been through an August football practice in full pads. That sauna became his office. While sitting faithfully by my side, he made recruiting calls and managed his enormous workload. I know it was hard on him, but it was a great comfort to see Hal as I slipped in and out of consciousness.

Sunday was a good day for me. Matt came by and Hal brought Leslie to see me. The Super Bowl was on, though I slept through most of the game. That day I tried to get up for the first time since the surgery. The abdominal incision that stretched from hip to hip was the prime source of pain during my recovery. When I tried to stand that day, the pain was unbearable. I learned I wouldn't be able to stand straight for four more weeks.

Super Bowl Sunday also was the first time Hal and I looked at the reconstructed right breast, my reduced left breast and my abdomen. Most of the transplanted tissue, which was comprised of muscle and fat, was used to create the size and contour of the breast. The incision around the skin and attached tissue was shaped like a football. There was still a lot of swelling. But the result was excellent. I was thrilled! Hal was smiling, too.

The reduction procedure had involved three incisions. One extends from the nipple down the center and the second begins under the breast near the center and extends outward. The third is around the areola. The result looked like the breast of a 20-year-old girl and I liked it!

Hal had initially been a little disappointed by my decision to reduce one breast to match the other. He had gotten used to the idea of a return to my former size 34DD. But he changed his mind when he saw the youthful appearance my new 34D breasts gave me.

The surgery has not returned me to pre-mastectomy days. My reconstructed breast doesn't feel like a natural one — its tissue is not as soft and I have no sensation in it. I also have no feeling in my belly button or parts of my tummy. Adjusting to the strange numbness took some time. And the physical results did not come without a heavy toll. There are no words to describe the intense pain and discomfort I experienced during the eight weeks of recovery after the flap procedure. Friends ask if it was worth the agony. My answer? Yes! Yes! Yes!

I feel like a whole woman again. My physical and emotional rebirth has been evident to everyone around me. Hal says I act like a new woman. I feel like one, too!

And I've noticed that Hal is acting like a new man. He's so cute. I think he's fallen in love all over again. I've always believed you don't just fall in love with someone once. I have re-fallen in love with Hal many times over, and I think he would say the same about me. It keeps our marriage new and exciting. I hope that never changes.

I was moved to a regular room at the Markey Cancer Center Monday morning, the same day Hal left town for a three-day recruiting trip.

The first day was difficult, but I did as well as could be expected. Tuesday, I was feeling much better. Several friends came to visit and I actually began to get restless. I was ready to go home and complete my recovery. Hal kept in constant touch by phone and was due back on Wednesday, in time for my release from the hospital. When he arrived to take me home, he was pleasantly surprised with my progress.

I was glad to have undergone the surgery in mid-winter. It was a good time of year to hibernate. I could spend the next several months convalescing at home and writing this book. Hal encouraged me to write about my experiences as an aid to my recovery. Some days I would work eight hours and others just 30 minutes, depending on how I felt. But every day, the writing stimulated me and made me feel better. I have taken great care to document my physical and emotional experiences in detail, and also to honestly communicate Hal's feelings. I hope this will help women, and the men who love them, deal with this devastating disease. Looking back, the best advice I could give to someone diagnosed with cancer is to gather all the information possible, then make decisions based on what is best for you.

My spirits were raised as I recovered that winter by Hal's recruiting successes. Each year the NCAA designates when high school seniors can officially sign a national letter-of-intent to document their choice of college. Hal was expecting to sign a great class on February 4, the start of the 1998 signing period.

A blizzard blew through most of Kentucky on the night of February 3, burying the state under more than a foot of snow. Hal could not even get out of the driveway the next morning, so he had to communicate by telephone with recruiting coordinator Claude Bassett. Claude called frequently to update Hal as faxes rolled in from players committing to Kentucky. At 10 a.m. the big news arrived. Alvis Johnson called from Harrodsburg to say his son, Dennis, had decided to be a Kentucky Wildcat. Dennis was the first lineman to be named Mr. Football in Kentucky. *USA Today*, *Parade* and the Atlanta Touchdown Club had picked him national prep defensive player of the year. Among the heavy hitters vying for his signature were Florida, Miami (Florida), Colorado and Notre Dame. But Dennis chose to anchor Hal's exceptional first full freshman class at Kentucky. He was thrilled.

Those thrilling days of limitless possibility have given way to the hard work that makes a champion. Our familiar cycle of preparation never ends. Recruiting and off-season conditioning leads to spring practice, which leads to summer training, then preseason practice in August, then yet another season. It takes a team effort to make it all work.

Claude Bassett never stops recruiting; he's forever sending letters, making phone calls and researching the next recruiting class. Mike Major and his defensive coaches prepare and plan workout schedules, depth charts and strategy. Mike Leach and Guy Morriss, under Hal's direction, do the same with the offense.

As I know from personal experience, no one's contributions to the Kentucky football program can be taken for granted, especially those of the assistant coaches' wives. They are the glue that holds their families together, patiently running the household to allow their husbands to focus on the team.

They are going through the same things I have experienced during a life spent with a football coach. I know that my strength and independence have allowed Hal the privilege of pursuing his dream. Had I not been there to keep the home fires burning, it would have been impossible for him to accomplish so much. I am the nurturer; I try to meet the emotional needs of the children and my husband, too, because he likes the attention. Hal and I have learned to defer to each other's strengths. And that makes our marriage work.

At Kentucky, we have a group of independent, talented wives with varied interests willing to support their husbands. That's the foundation of a good team.

We also have an uncommonly strong man leading the program. It amazes me that Hal did his job so well last year while helping me battle breast cancer and its devastating aftermath. Even as he took on his greatest challenge, he was always there for me. Though he spent long hours at my side and on the phone with me, I never saw any signs he wasn't focusing on football, too. It was such a marvelous balancing act; he never showed any stress or strain. He handled whatever needed to be done, whether for me or for the football program. That's just the way he is. I'm certain it was Hal's talent at setting priorities that allowed him to navigate through such the maze of mounting responsibilities. Our marriage is a gift I will treasure always. I feel so lucky to be sharing my life with this man.

And I gladly share Hal with his players and the community because, in my heart, I know that coaching is his greatest gift of all. I'm lucky enough to see the behind-the-scenes skills that go unnoticed by most fans. Hal's leadership, organizational ability and motivational savvy are more fascinating to me than the technical strategies for which he's renowned. What I know is the obvious: his passing game is high entertainment, even for those of us who lack great knowledge of the game. It's thrilling to watch the ball sail through the air, a receiver soaring for the catch and bolting for extra yardage. It's fun to score.

You can count on Hal's teams to do just that. He will tell you he's a coach of a football team. But I would argue that he's really a catalyst to great memories — for the players, fans and university. We're all members of the team. We learn to contribute, cooperate, set goals and achieve our dreams together. It's critical in our everyday life.

I never worry about winning and losing. I know we will ultimately prevail, because Hal, his capable staff, the hard-working players, and the supportive university have put themselves in position to win.

After the game is over and the stadium lights are turned off, we'll tuck our memories away for future use. Hal and I already have an attic full of rich recollections from a full and happy life. And we're thrilled to be in the early pages of this exciting chapter. The great memories at the University of Kentucky have only begun.